Great Buildings of the World

ABBEYS OF EUROPE

by Ian Richards

PAUL HAMLYN

PUBLISHED BY THE HAMLYN PUBLISHING GROUP LIMITED,
HAMLYN HOUSE, THE CENTRE, FELTHAM, MIDDLESEX

Printed and made in Great Britain by
Thomas Nelson (Printers) Ltd, London and Edinburgh

Endpapers: *From a 19th-century engraving of the ruins of Kirkstall Abbey, Yorkshire.*

Frontispiece: *The 15th-century chapter house at Maulbronn, the Cistercian abbey founded in Württemberg in 1147.*

Contents

INTRODUCTION

FROM ST BENEDICT TO CLUNY

There are several reasons why monastic architecture has a claim on our interest. First, monasteries are very large and complex undertakings, involving problems of planning as well as of design (during the middle ages they were the largest architectural units in existence); secondly, they provide a continuous tradition of challenge and response that has been met in every style and in every country during the whole of the Christian era; and finally they represent a way of life that is (whether one sympathises with it or not) a spiritual quest, a complete personal commitment to which many of the most brilliant men and women of the last 1500 years have dedicated themselves. This alone makes a monastery—to most people—more interesting than an office block. For no building can be understood or appreciated purely as 'architecture'; one has to know why it was built and how it was used. This is why this book begins with a short account of the origins of monasticism, its ideals and early history, and describes briefly the constitutions of the various orders as they occur.

'There was once a man of venerable life whose name was Benedict; and Blessed [*benedictus*] he was in grace as well as in name. From his very boyhood he had the wisdom of age, for with a virtue beyond his years he surrendered his heart to no worldly pleasure. Although he might, as far as this world goes, have enjoyed these pleasures freely, yet he despised the barren delights of the world and spurned its allurements.' So begins Gregory the Great's *Life of St Benedict* (our only source) and so begins the history of Western monasticism.

St Benedict was born at Nursia, near Spoleto in Italy, about 480. His family was noble, and he spent the first twenty years of his life in Rome, receiving the best available education, which was still

A 15th-century French manuscript depicting monks singing in a choir. Prayer was the most important activity in any monastery and monks attended seven services a day and one at night.

basically the education of the classical world as modified by Christianity. But Rome at this time was already a city living on its past. In 330 Constantine had moved the imperial capital to Constantinople, and in 402 the Western emperor Honorius, under threat of barbarian attack, had abandoned Rome and moved to Ravenna. Rome was in fact sacked by the Visigoths in 410. In 476 the last of the Western emperors was deposed at Ravenna, which a few years later fell to the Ostrogoths under Theodoric.

Theodoric saw himself as an emperor in the old style. When he visited Rome in 500 the patricians assembled into a 'senate' to welcome him, games were held and free grain distributed to the poor. (Benedict was then a young man of about 20.) But it was a precarious empire. After Theodoric's death the Ostrogothic kings failed completely to hold it together and it was reconquered piecemeal by the Byzantines. Totila, the last Ostrogothic king, is supposed

Western monasticism began at Montecassino, below. First built about 530, it has been repeatedly destroyed and rebuilt—most recently in 1943. This view shows it as it looked before the Second World War—a collection of buildings of every date, majestically crowning its wooded hill. It was here that St Benedict brought his companions in 529 and wrote the Rule, which has been the basis of monastic life ever since.

Cum domibus miris plutei parata accipe libros.

Left, St Benedict seated and holding the Rule blesses his 11th-century successor Desiderius, under whom Montecassino rose to its most splendid achievements. Desiderius is donating books (some of which lie at his feet) and landed estates (at the bottom of the picture) to the abbey. The architectural background is probably meant to stand for the monastery.

Overleaf, a plan of St Gall, redrawn and simplified from the ninth-century original in the monastery library of St Gall in Switzerland. Nothing as completely regular as this was ever built, and was probably never intended to be. It does give, however, a more complete 'programme' for a monastery than any actual remains.

to have visited Benedict in his old age at Montecassino. Less than twenty years later the reconquest was again reversed by the Lombard invasion (568). It was the beginning of the so-called dark ages, a period of large-scale migrations—first the Goths, Lombards, Vandals and Huns, and then the Moors in the west, the Vikings in the north, the Slavs and Magyars in the east—which lasted until the 11th century and made stable government almost impossible. (Charlemagne's empire represents a brief respite, but he was continually at war on one frontier or another.) In such conditions the tightly knit, disciplined, self-supporting communities following the Benedictine Rule were able to survive better than any other social unit. It would be misleading to suggest that Benedict foresaw these

11

developments; what is certain is that his planning enabled them to carry on during this difficult period.

St Benedict's own early instincts seem to have been in favour of withdrawal from the world, a course for which there was plenty of precedent. 'Monasticism' in this sense had begun in Egypt, where individual hermit-monks sought their own path to salvation, some of them eccentric to the point of mania. A certain amount of organisation was introduced by St Pachomius and St Basil, who founded communities under the direction of a superior; such loosely organised monasteries spread all over Europe and often became firmly established. The monasteries of Celtic Ireland and Scotland during the sixth and seventh centuries were of this kind, and they did not submit to the Benedictine model without a struggle.

St Benedict, then, turned his back on Rome and retired to a lonely spot in the mountains where he lived for three years on his own. A band of disciples, however, eventually gathered round him; these he formed into groups of 12, each under a superior, but all under his supervision. About the year 530 he and his monks moved south to Montecassino, a magnificent hill-top site between Rome and Naples. Here he abandoned the idea of small separate groups and brought all his followers together into one community. The position of Montecassino itself, which, far from being a remote sanctuary, is (unhappily, as it turned out during the Second World War) strategically placed near a main highway, is another sign of the way his thoughts were evolving. It was soon, according to Gregory's *Life*, a busy centre for preaching, alms-giving, nursing and teaching. Here Benedict worked out the details of his system and wrote the Rule, which is the foundation of all succeeding Western monasticism.

The *Rule of St Benedict* is fundamental to an appreciation of the subject of this book; unfortunately there is not room to quote from it at length. It is very easy to read, very simple and specific. Every monk must have known it practically by heart, and for real insight into the purpose and function of monastic buildings it is more valuable than any number of guide-books.

It has two basic principles: work and prayer. Life is completely communal. Private property is abolished. Everyone is equal. Each man has his task and does it: 'Here! Work, and be sad no longer.' The monastery is a profit-making concern. It does not beg—it gives. No individual may benefit from his labours but (and here lay the seeds of corruption) the house as a whole may. Compared with earlier monastic codes, the emphasis is on moderation. Not too much

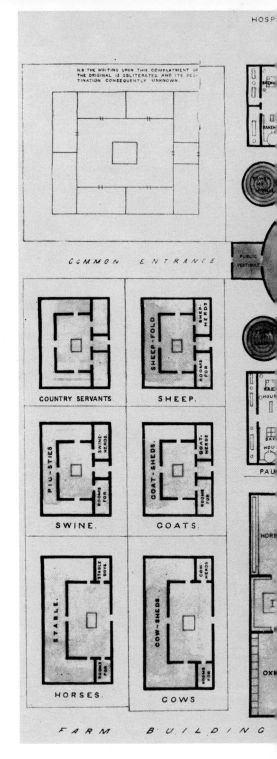

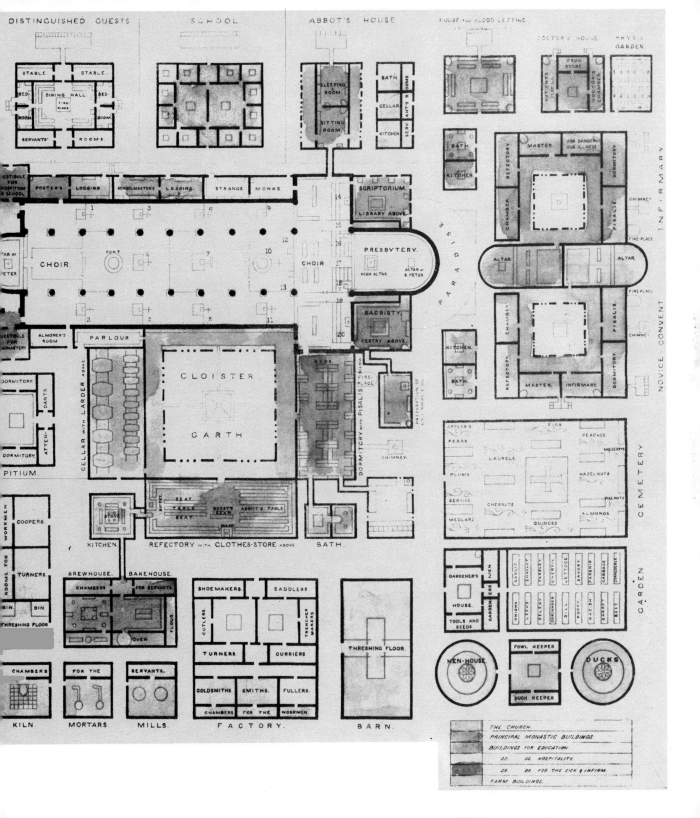

comfort, but not too much austerity either; the exercise of piety combined with a healthy concern for survival.

After defining its general principles the Rule continues by laying down specific regulations for every hour of the day and every department of the monastery. It is an amazingly detailed scheme, though not fanatically rigid. Benedict, indeed, never seems to have considered himself as the founder of an order. His Rule was meant for Montecassino only. Others could adopt it if they chose—and this remained the position for several centuries.

The monk, after a period of probation, took vows of obedience, conversion of life and stability; that is, he promised to obey the abbot, to strive for moral perfection and to remain in his monastery for the rest of his life. Poverty and chastity are not explicitly enjoined though they are certainly implied. But poverty for St Benedict meant giving up private possessions, not the absolute penury embraced by St Francis.

From our point of view, the most relevant parts of the Rule are those concerned with the running of the monastery: the arrangement of the dormitories, hours of sleep, numbers of lights to be kept burning; the times of meals, what is to be eaten and how much, cooking, serving; caring for the sick; the entertainment of guests; distribution of charity; amount and type of clothing, laundry and extra clothes for journeys; rules for novices and new members; punishments; delegation of authority (the abbot was elected by the monks and although sovereign was expected to consult them before taking any important decision); the upkeep of the church and buildings; security against attack and so on. St Benedict omits nothing. To take one small example to illustrate his minute attention to detail: Chapter 38, the rules for reading aloud during meals.

> 'There ought always to be reading whilst the brethren are at table. . . . The greatest silence shall be kept, so that no whispering nor noise save the voice of the reader alone be heard there. Whatever is required for eating or drinking the brethren shall minister to each other so that no one need ask for anything. . . . The brother who is reader for the week may take a mess of pottage before beginning to read, lest perchance it may be too long for him to fast. He shall eat afterwards with the weekly servers and kitchen helpers. Not all the brethren are to take turns in reading, but only such as may edify the hearers.'

The most fundamental part of the monk's daily life is prayer.

His day is punctuated by ceremonial. There are eight services—seven during the day, one at night. (The inspiration for this scheme is Psalm CXIX—'Seven times a day do I praise thee. . . . At midnight I will rise to give thanks to thee'.) St Benedict recommends that the prayers should be short, though the whole Psalter is to be read once a week. In addition every monk should engage in constant private prayer, upon which he offers some illuminating advice but makes no regulations.

While reading the Rule one can almost see the monastic layout taking shape. Like a castle, its form grows out of its function. The monks need a church, readily accessible—each of them has to go in and out of it eight times a day. They need a big room to eat together; another in which to sleep. They need a kitchen, an infirmary, storehouse and meeting-place. All these rooms have to be in easy communication with one another, and there has to be plenty of passageway since everybody in a monastery is perpetually on the move. So the standard plan, with the various buildings grouped round a square cloister protected from the weather, seems to evolve spontaneously. And this layout hardly changed for the next thousand years.

Having said this, it is interesting to note the classical roots of many monastic elements. For instance, it has been pointed out that monasteries (especially new ones founded in remote territory) have much in common with Roman *coloniae*, towns for retired veterans. One is also reminded of Diocletian's palace at Split, which in its planning might be called an imperial secular monastery. The church is a development from the Roman basilica. The cloister is the Roman atrium. The drainage and water-supply are likely to be arranged on Roman military principles. (Sewage disposal is not the least striking of the aspects of the classical heritage preserved by the monasteries during the middle ages.) Indeed, it might be claimed that monasticism itself, with its emphasis on efficiency and expansion, is the Roman idea of discipline transposed on to a spiritual plane. And is not the abbot, autocratic but benign, the Roman *paterfamilias*? These comparisons are not merely fanciful: St Benedict was more of an 'antique Roman' than a man of the middle ages, and monastic culture is in essence only classical culture under siege.

But how much of this is true of the first foundation at Montecassino? No one can tell. About 580 the Lombards sacked it. The monks fled to Rome, where they were allowed by the pope to live in a monastery next to the Lateran. Here they remained for about

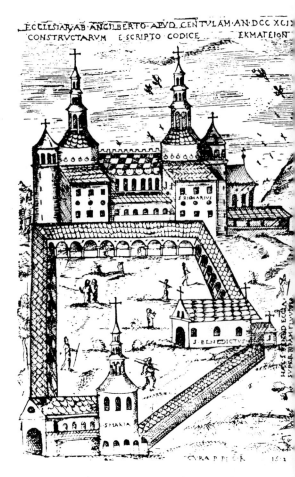

Above, an old drawing (itself recopied from an earlier document) of the abbey of Centula, near Abbeville in northern France, which gives some idea of its original appearance. (All trace of it has vanished.) Dating from about 790, Centula was among the great abbeys built as part of Charlemagne's conscious programme of extending monastic power and influence.

The abbot was the head and father of the monastic community. Opposite, a relief (c. 1100) showing the Abbot Durandus of Moissac, his right hand raised in blessing, his left grasping his pastoral staff.

15

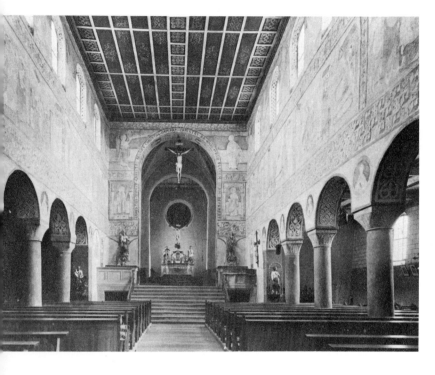

140 years. Pope Gregory the Great, author of the *Life of St Benedict*, became one of them and founded a monastery in Rome, St Andrew the Apostle, whose constitution seems to have followed the Benedictine Rule. This monastery was an extremely important foundation. St Augustine of Canterbury was once prior and only left it (unwillingly) to accomplish the conversion of England.

By these and similar missions during the late sixth and early seventh centuries the Rule spread to France and England, where more and more monasteries adopted it and lived by it. Often it was modified or combined with other rules. This was not an age of standardisation—a monk did not join an order, he joined a house. Nor were all the monasteries that followed St Benedict's Rule united administratively in any way; each managed its own affairs.

By the late seventh century a clearer pattern begins to emerge. At the Synod of Whitby (664) it was decided to introduce the Rule in all English monasteries. Missionaries from England carried it to Germany and Scandinavia (where Christianity and the Rule arrived together). By the eighth century it was generally adopted in Spain.

Reichenau, Insula Felix, had three important monasteries. The best preserved is Oberzell, where the church of St George (seen above left), dating originally from 836, still preserves a complete series of Ottonian frescoes. Reichenau was famous for its art and scholarship.

FVLDENSIS CIVITATIS, & *celeberrimæ abbatiæ eiusdem imago.*

Charlemagne and his successors gave it official support, and the other varieties of monasticism virtually disappeared in the West.

Meanwhile the fortunes of Montecassino had been chequered. The monks returned early in the eighth century and rebuilt their monastery, only to see it sacked again in 884, this time by the Saracens. About 950 rebuilding began once more on a large scale, and now at last we can reconstruct something of its physical appearance. Before doing so, however, it may be helpful to look at some of the earlier abbeys of which traces have survived.

Hardly anything remains of buildings before the age of Charlemagne, though we know from documents and chronicles that they must have been growing in numbers and in strength. In many parts of Europe they provided the only stable element in society when effective government broke down. They were enriched by endowments and gifts of land. They grew on the patronage of princes and they survived when the princes perished. In an age, too, of economic disorder the monks acquired crucial importance as agriculturalists and managers.

A late-16th-century woodcut depicting the great Carolingian abbey of Fulda, in Germany, which was among the leading monastic centres of the early middle ages. Here the relics of St Boniface, the apostle to the Germans, were brought after his death in 754. The church was modelled on old St Peter's, and the whole monastery completed by 822.

17

The monasteries were already the only centres of education and art. Their schools trained the diplomats and civil servants of Europe; their scriptoria kept alive a knowledge of classical literature. When Charlemagne (crowned Emperor of the West on Christmas Day 800) began his programme of cultural revival it was on the monasteries that he relied most heavily.

One of Charlemagne's leading advisers, Angilbert, dedicated the Abbey of Centula in France in 799. The church was basilican, about 250 feet long, with an atrium in front of it about 90 feet square and a 'westwork' at the west end. There were two crossings, each with a tower, and other towers along the transepts. The buildings have all disappeared but on the evidence of a drawing made from a manuscript of 1088 (which was destroyed in 1719) the monastery was on a monumental scale. The cloister, which is curiously described as 'triangular', had two chapels opening from it; the layout of the other buildings is unknown.

The most complete picture of what an abbey of this period would have been like can be gained from a monastery-that-never-was: the plan drawn in about 820 and now in the Library of St Gall. Where and why it was made are not definitely known. Most probably it was

Angilbert's grandiose abbey at Centula was soon imitated in other parts of Charlemagne's Empire. In 822 a party of monks from Picardy founded Corvey, on the Weser, and gave their church a 'westwork' on the lines of Centula. Its spacious interior, left, is not unworthy of the ancient Roman models that its builders sought to emulate.

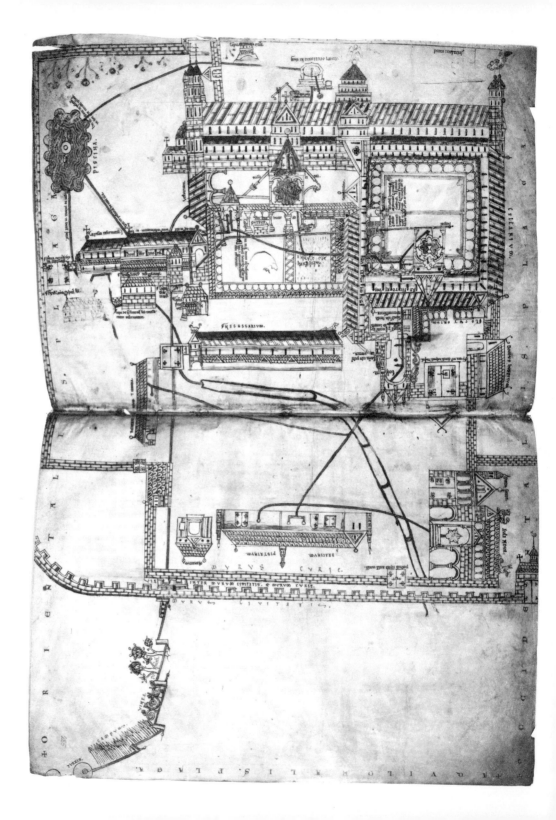

sent by the Abbot of Reichenau to the Abbot of St Gall after a council held in 816 at which the latter was not present. But whatever the explanation, it gives a sort of blueprint for a standard layout, arranged with perhaps artificial regularity but containing everything needed for a working monastery. The Abbey of St Gall was in fact built, but apparently according to a different plan.

The layout of the church itself is basically similar to that at Centula. The monastic buildings are arranged on what was by then evidently the traditional plan: a cloister on the south side of the nave (which thus forms its north side) and on the other three sides the dormitory (east), refectory (south) and cellar (west). The monks' entrance to the church was via the south transept.

The details of life as it was expected to be led at St Gall can be reconstructed with great precision. In the dormitory, for instance, the way the beds were to be placed is shown, as were the tables and

Above, the chapter house of Bristol, dating from the mid-12th century. The door and two windows lead into the cloister. The walls are covered in lively Romanesque decoration, and the vault carried on thick ribs carved with a double zigzag.

Opposite, the Canterbury plan (referred to on p. 26). The lines running through it show the course of the pipes, which bring the water in at the bottom from a natural spring some miles away, serve various parts of the monastic buildings (including two fountain-houses, the infirmary, the kitchen and the fish pond), and lead out again, bottom right, after draining the necessarium. 21

benches in the refectory. By studying the chimneys one can deduce which rooms were to be heated and by noting the latrines which sections were to be self-contained. The number of farm buildings and the variety of services that could be carried out within the monastery itself (including threshing, grinding and baking, brewing and even the making of barrels) are reminiscent of a feudal manor. The infirmary and the novices' quarters, east of the church, are again little worlds of their own, while lavish attention is paid to charity, hospitality and education. The church and claustral buildings would doubtless have been of stone, most of the others of wood.

One of the greatest monastic centres of Charlemagne's empire was the island of Reichenau in Lake Constance. It had three monasteries—Niederzell, Mittelzell and Oberzell. The churches still survive, that of Oberzell with a superb series of Carolingian frescoes, and some at least of the monastic buildings can be reconstructed. Mittelzell had the usual cloister beside the nave with the main gate, somewhat surprisingly, opening into it, and a spacious atrium in front of the west end. This was a feature taken from such early Christian churches as Old St Peter's. The 'paradise' at St Gall was a development from this.

There were certainly many more equally magnificent monasteries. The chronicles speak of fine buildings, splendid services and costly

vessels. Of these little remain, though here and there the plan of a church can be recovered. Fulda, in Germany, was rebuilt in 790 on a plan similar to that of Centula. The Abbey of Lorsch, near the Rhine, was a large and important foundation added to by Charlemagne and undoubtedly in his grandest imperial style. The so-called Gatehouse is among the best preserved of Carolingian buildings but its position in the monastic complex is difficult to decide.

One of the most interesting figures of the late 10th and early 11th centuries is William of Volpiano. His high position was partly due to the eminence of his family (he had relatives in many ruling houses of Europe and his godmother was an empress) but mainly to his energy and vision. He joined Cluny in 987 and from there went to Dijon to reform the monastery of St Bénigne, which he did very effectively. In the early 11th century he was in Normandy revitalising the monastic tradition there (he founded the famous Abbey of Bec). His architectural work was as original as his other activities and he made his church at Dijon into 'the most wonderful of all the churches in Gaul'. Over 300 feet long, it had double aisles and was stone-vaulted throughout, and it ended (behind the altar) in a large rotunda based on the Holy Sepulchre at Jerusalem. This had a certain influence among equally ardent spirits (for example, Wulfric's rotunda at Canterbury in 1050), though it was too personal to pass into the mainstream of architectural history. Today only the crypt survives.

Montecassino, to which we now return, was meanwhile being rebuilt on a scale suitable to its importance. By the mid-11th century under the great abbot Desiderius (1058–87) it must have been an imposing sight on its hill-top. In front of the church was a square atrium, or 'paradise'. The dormitory was on the south of the cloister and its more normal position on the east was given up to a large chapter house, a room that usually occupied the ground floor of the dormitory wing. The refectory was on the west. The church was consecrated with the greatest ceremony in 1071 and Desiderius laboured to make his monastery a religious and cultural centre for the whole of Italy. He is even said (by his friend and biographer Leo of Ostia) to have brought artists over from Byzantium. Whether he also imported the pointed arch is a question on which architectural historians disagree.

The monastic movement was now (in the late 11th century) surging forward with renewed energy. In England there were the new foundations of the Normans. In Germany monasteries acted as

Above, the kitchen at Glastonbury Abbey, where the octagonal vault rests on a square base, leaving the four corners open for the chimneys from the four ovens to emerge. Lighting was by a central lantern.

Far left, the gatehouse of Bury St Edmunds, all that survives in anything like recognisable shape of the great Benedictine abbey. It is a splendid example of Norman work, four storeys high, built about 1130. In this view we are looking from inside the abbey precinct.

Centre, a particularly elaborate pulpit at the old Cistercian monastery of Beaulieu in Hampshire, now the parish church. From here a monk would read to the other brethren during meals. 23

Left, the ceiling of the kitchen at Durham (similar in plan to that of Glastonbury), which has an interesting pattern of vaulting ribs to support it.

Right, the big austere church at Gernrode. At ground level columns alternate with piers, and at gallery level each double bay is given a row of six small arches. Monasteries could be the outposts of Christianity on the frontiers of paganism. The Slavs to the east of Otto I's empire were still being Christianised when Gernrode was founded in 961.

Left, Montecassino as it probably looked in 1075, reconstructed by Professor Kenneth Conant. The church with its atrium lies on the left; beside it is the cloister with the chapter house (far side) and dormitory (the long building on the right) opening from it. The west range consists (in diminishing order of size) of the refectory, novices' quarters and kitchen. It was this monastery that Abbot Hugh of Cluny visited in 1083.

mission outposts against the pagan Slavs, and in Spain as the crusader castles of the *Reconquista*, the centuries-long struggle to win back the peninsula from the Moors. Mountain-abbeys like St Martin-du-Canigou show that the old ideals of seclusion had not faded; while a foundation like Ripoll, not many miles distant, provides evidence of more worldly ambitions. Ripoll was begun in 1020 under Abbot Oliba, a leading figure in the Church and state. It was a grandiose enterprise, a huge church with double aisles and (in parts) a stone vault, frescoes on the wall, jewels on the altar, mosaics on the floor. Its school and scriptorium were soon famous. In 1046 its library contained 246 volumes.

By now in fact, the character of monasticism was again changing. Europe had weathered the storms of the dark ages. Life outside the cloister was likely to be hardly more turbulent than life inside. Monasteries were no longer oases of peace, security and devotion in an alien world. Their riches, however piously acquired and laudably spent, inevitably made them powerful. Abbots were likely to be men of influence, ecclesiastics as well as fathers, and politicians as well as ecclesiastics.

These larger considerations of the place of monasticism in medieval society take us outside the scope of this book. It is necessary to make the point, however, in order to understand the later developments within monasticism. For, to put it at its simplest, the remainder of monastic history until the Reformation is the story of repeated attempts to get away from involvement in the world, to renounce worldly success and return to the simplicity of Benedict's Rule.

The daily life of a 12th-century monk is better documented than that of almost any other member of society. We can follow him, in the 'Customs' or 'Uses' that were compiled for the larger houses, from his getting up in the morning to his going to bed at night. For the architectural historian it is usually fairly easy to relate these descriptions to the buildings as they survive, and we shall try to do this for some of the abbeys that follow. In one case, however, we can do even better. There is at Trinity College, Cambridge, a pictorial plan of the monastery of Christchurch, Canterbury, made about 1165 in connection with a new water-supply. It is, of course, concerned only with the more practical aspects of monastic life, but within its limits it gives as vivid and complete a picture for the 12th century as the St Gall plan did for the ninth—with the advantage that the monastery at Canterbury was actually built and in fact stands in great part today.

26

It was a large monastery, with two cloisters and numbers of subsidiary buildings. In the old plan the church is at the top and we are looking at it from the north. On the right, below the nave (that is, next to its north side), is the large cloister, clearly shown by its four covered arcades. On its east side are the chapter house (*Capitulum*) and dormitory (*Dormitorium*), on the west the cellarer's range and guests' rooms (*Cellarium*) and on the north—here one is obliged to turn the drawing upside-down to read it—is the refectory (*Refectorium*) with behind it the kitchen (*Coquina*). The elaborate structure in front of the refectory is the fountain where the monks washed before meals. The kitchen is shown in considerable detail. A curvilinear pattern at one side of it represents a vine growing up the wall. On the other side is an apse-shaped projection labelled

The frontier with the Moors in Spain was just as unsettled as that with the eastern Slavs. Here too monasteries were bastions of the faith. San Pedro de Roda, above, was one of those built under the leadership of the great abbot Oliba of Ripoll. It was consecrated in 1022, its castellated walls commanding a strategic position near Gerona.

Opposite, a view looking east from the remains of the north aisle of Hersfeld, through the crossing into the narrower chancel with its apsed ending. Hersfeld, dating in its present form from 1037, is typical of the scale of German abbey-churches with their relatively rich patronage.

27

Camera ubi piscis lavatur ('chamber where the fish is washed'). Between kitchen and refectory is a short passage with two windows labelled *Fenestra ubi fercula administrantur* ('window at which the portions are served out') and *Fenestra per quam ejiciuntur scutelle ad lavandum* ('window through which the dishes are thrown out for washing').

To the east of the large cloister (to its left in the drawing, on the other side of the dormitory) is a smaller cloister. It too is surrounded by an arcaded walk, the south side of which is labelled *Via que ducit ad domum infirmorum* ('passage leading to the infirmary'). The large structure standing in the middle of this side (it looks very like the fountain-house by the refectory, but is drawn the other way up) is the main cistern of the whole monastery; here the water was collected and distributed to all the other parts.

This smaller cloister is divided into two by a fence and the ground on one side planted with herbs (*herbarium*). Continuing east, we reach the infirmary, which has its own dormitory, chapel, kitchen and latrine (*Necessarium infirmorum*) exactly as at St Gall, though on a different plan. The main *necessarium* for the whole abbey is at the bottom of the drawing, a long separate range with 11 windows. The water, having served a variety of purposes, flows out through this range to the river. Like most of the other buildings at Canterbury, it can still easily be recognised today.

Canterbury, indeed, is still a fairly well-preserved ensemble, though none of its component parts, as they now exist, is particularly noteworthy. Elsewhere, it often happens that one part survives in a good state when the rest has totally disappeared. No single Romanesque monastery containing outstanding examples of every feature now exists, so it may be useful, in this introductory chapter, to note a few features that are not so well represented later. For the sake of consistency the list is confined to English examples.

Most Benedictine houses had a strong entrance gate and the finest still extant is that of Bury St Edmunds, a great abbey that has otherwise almost entirely vanished. It is a massive affair, built about 1130, with a gabled archway flanked by turrets and rising to a height of four storeys, not unlike a miniature Norman keep.

Of Romanesque cloisters hardly anything survives—a sad state of affairs when one thinks of the riches possessed by France, Spain and Germany. For chapter houses we have to go to Bristol, which has a superb room of two bays, decorated with the most lavish geometrical ornament; or to Worcester, where it is circular and covered by a

The monastery of St Martin-du-Canigou, on a hilltop in the Pyrenees, has one of the most picturesque sites in Europe. In the early 12th century the monks had a serious reason for choosing it and the strong battlemented tower behind the church served the same purpose as the keep of a castle. The cloister clings to the south side of the church, with dormitory and refectory ranged on its east and west.

vault radiating from one central pillar. (Worcester stands at the beginning of a uniquely English development—the polygonal chapter house—which culminates in the magnificent examples at Lincoln, Salisbury, Westminster, Wells and York.) There are no well-preserved Norman refectories, though those of Chester and Beaulieu may be placed fairly early in the 13th century. Two fine kitchens are still to be seen at Durham and Glastonbury, though again they are rather later than the period we are discussing. Durham also has an impressive dormitory (now the cathedral museum), while a complete flight of 'night' stairs, by which the monks descended from the dormitory to the church, survives at Hexham. Castle Acre has a row of monks' latrines in a good state of preservation. Romanesque infirmaries have again mostly perished, though a good idea of their form can be gained from Canterbury and Ely. They were very like

31

churches with aisles and chancels, but no transepts. The 'nave' was the main space of the infirmary, the 'aisles' contained beds or (later) cubicles, and the 'chancel' was the chapel, usually opening directly into the infirmary through a wooden screen. At Ely most of these parts are still standing, though incorporated into later buildings in a way that may diminish their archaeological value but certainly adds to their charm.

This introduction may fitly close with an account of the rise of the Cluniacs, a story that exemplifies both the glories of medieval monasticism and the subtle way in which its original values were compromised. The beginnings of Cluny (in Burgundy) go back to 909 when a group of monks took over a Gallo-Roman villa and built themselves a church. It was under Odo, who became abbot in 927, that its real greatness began. Odo was a saintly and apparently very charming man, who had found in the Benedictine Rule the most perfect guide to salvation and whose only wish was to establish it as widely as possible in its strictest and most orthodox form. He was so successful at Cluny that the pope invited him to reform several other important monasteries in Italy as well as France. Several houses thus came under his supervision and were at the same time 'exempted' from interference by the local bishops; this control continued to be exercised by Odo's successors. Gradually the idea of a Cluniac 'congregation' grew up, a network of monasteries under one central authority. The man at the head of this network was powerful. Odo, the saint, had acted like a statesman. But it was an innovation quite unforeseen by St Benedict.

A new church (known as Cluny II) was dedicated in 981; the monastic buildings were systematically rebuilt on a grand scale and the whole was finished by about 1040. It had a large west court with stables, guests' lodgings and an infirmary; a novices' cloister, complete with all the normal features; and of course all the usual claustral buildings arranged on the standard plan. Cluny even then was famous for its music. It had an important library, scriptorium and even a goldsmith's and enameller's shop.

Fifty years later the monastery had again outgrown its buildings. Abbot Hugh (1049–1103) enlarged it enormously; he rebuilt the church (Cluny III) to enormous dimensions, pulling down the old nave and incorporating the resulting space in the cloister, and added many other buildings on a similar scale. The whole complex covered over 25 acres. When Pope Innocent IV, Louis IX of France and the Emperor of Constantinople all met at Cluny in 1245 the

Right and overleaf, three capitals from Romanesque cloisters. It was carvings such as these that aroused St Bernard's hostility in the 12th century. From the Cistercian point of view they represented money wasted and ingenuity misapplied, since they served rather to distract than to aid contemplation. The capital, right, showing harpies (birds with women's heads) and oriental lions, is from the Spanish monastery of Silos, and dates from about 1100.

Two capitals directly influenced by Cluny. The first from Vézelay, left, displays a devil riding on a griffin; the second from Autun, right, shows the Temptation, treated with all the dramatic energy of the sculptor Gislebertus.

monastery was able to accommodate some 2000 guests without disturbing the monks.

By now Cluny's influence had spread far and wide, both directly, by the founding of daughter-houses, and indirectly, by the other houses who adopted the Cluniac reforms and submitted to Cluniac authority. At its peak, it has been calculated, the Abbot of Cluny controlled about 1500 monasteries; he was second only to the pope in the hierarchy of Christendom (four popes, indeed, came from the ranks of Cluny). His town house in Paris, the Hôtel de Cluny, survives as evidence of his prestige.

Cluny itself in the 12th century must have been a magnificent sight. Abbot Hugh's great church, bigger than any cathedral then standing, had double aisles, two pairs of transepts, a chevet of chapels at the east end, tunnel vaulting and, in the arcades of the nave, pointed arches. A hugh fresco of Christ in Glory gazed down from the apse and the church was filled with superb sculpture of which a few capitals representing the Virtues, the Seasons and the 'tones' of plainsong are almost all that remain. 'Among all the abbeys beyond the Alps', said Gregory VII at the Council of Rome in 1077, 'there shines first and foremost that of Cluny.'

The monks of Cluny were the élite of the monastic world, and while their labours were devoted, they were not manual. Cluny became more and more an intellectual and artistic centre that depended for its maintenance on an army of servants, like any other grand estate. The monks occupied themselves with a liturgy of unusual beauty and elaboration. Devotional poetry flourished, preserved in exquisitely written manuscripts. The church absorbed the energies of the best sculptors of France, who later took the style evolved here to such abbeys as Vézelay and Autun, where it has survived better than at the mother-house. Its architecture too was emulated, though not so much in France as in England, where there were a number of houses owing allegiance to Cluny.

In many ways these developments were of tremendous benefit. It was in one sense the great age of the monasteries. Never again would they be such a power in politics, so rich, so lavish in their patronage, so splendid in the works that they created for the glory of God. Yet already men within the monastic movement were asking more and more insistently whether their lives were really consistent with the spirit of St Benedict's teaching. If not, what ought to be done? It was a question to be answered in uncompromising terms by St Bernard.

CHAPTER 1

NORWICH:
THE BENEDICTINES IN ENGLAND

Like many of the most important Benedictine abbeys of England, Norwich was also a cathedral. The titular abbot was the bishop, but he was not a member of the monastery, except in a few cases. Normally he was a nominee of the king (once of the pope) and he lived in a palace with his own establishment. The monastery was in charge of the prior, who was abbot in all but name. Not surprisingly, bishop and prior spent much of their time and energy disagreeing with each other.

Cathedral-priories, as they were called, were an invention of the Normans. The foundation of Norwich is dated 1094, when the see was moved from Thetford (there had been a previous Saxon bishopric at Elmham). The bishop who took the decision, and who is therefore called the founder of Norwich, was Herbert de Losinga, a man in whom shrewdness and ambition took precedence over piety. He paid William Rufus £1900 for his own appointment as Bishop of Norwich (or Thetford as it then was) and for his father's as Bishop of Winchester. 'I entered on mine office disgracefully', he confessed candidly some years later, 'but by the help of God's grace I shall pass out of it with credit'—a hope that one might say has been fulfilled.

Norman bishops in general were key figures in the political structure and their appointments were made with this in mind. They were men of action rather than saints. Their function was to make a clean sweep of Anglo-Saxon monasticism and to build up the new Norman foundations into centres of power and influence.

Monasticism in Normandy at this time was rejoicing in a burst of energy stemming from Burgundy (William of Volpiano's dynamic presence being the prime mover), which led to the foundation of

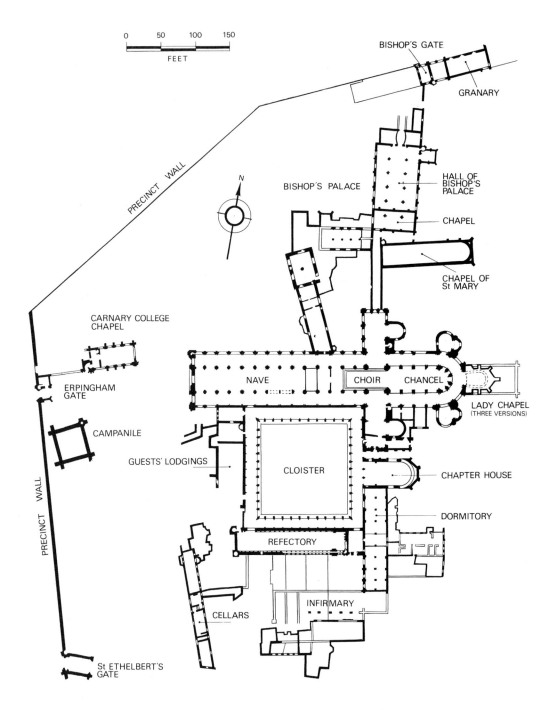

0   50   100   150
FEET

BISHOP'S GATE

GRANARY

PRECINCT WALL

N

BISHOP'S PALACE

HALL OF BISHOP'S PALACE

CHAPEL

CHAPEL OF St MARY

CARNARY COLLEGE CHAPEL

ERPINGHAM GATE

CAMPANILE

GUESTS' LODGINGS

PRECINCT WALL

NAVE

CHOIR   CHANCEL

LADY CHAPEL (THREE VERSIONS)

CHAPTER HOUSE

CLOISTER

DORMITORY

REFECTORY

INFIRMARY

CELLARS

St ETHELBERT'S GATE

A plan showing the position of the cathedral and monastic buildings at Norwich.

great abbeys like Fécamp, Jumièges, Bec and Caen. It was from these forcing houses of monastic talent that the abbots and bishops of Norman England were to be recruited. Lanfranc, the new Archbishop of Canterbury had been Abbot of Bec and Prior of St Etienne at Caen. Herbert de Losinga himself had been Abbot of Fécamp. He began his cathedral at Norwich in 1096. He started at the east end, as was the usual practice, and the choir he built was modelled quite closely on his old abbey at Fécamp. It had an apse, ambulatory and three radiating chapels. The middle chapel, which has been rebuilt at least twice, was apparently conventional enough, but a typically English anomaly appears in the other two. When chapels radiate from a semicircle they cannot all, of course, point due east; some point north-east or south-east. This ritual impurity evidently worried the English builders, so two strange little apses are added to the east side of the already curved chapels, giving them a most extraordinary plan. It succeeded however in orientating all the altars. A similar solution is found at Canterbury.

When Herbert de Losinga died in 1119 the church had probably progressed as far as the first three or four bays of the nave. That is, there were standing the choir, with its three chapels; the transepts, each also with an eastern chapel; and the crossing tower as far as the level of the choir roof. At this point there are signs of a pause in building, but it cannot have been prolonged and the next bishop, Everard (1121–45), is recorded as having completed the church, which would have been covered by a wooden ceiling like Ely or Peterborough. The monastic buildings were erected at the same time as the church and certainly more quickly—many of them during de Losinga's lifetime. Since these have for the most part disappeared, it is necessary to refer to the plan to appreciate their extent.

The heart of the monastery was the cloister, and we may begin our description at the north-east corner, where the monks would normally enter and leave it from the church. At Norwich this doorway is a magnificent 14th-century work known as the Prior's Door. Proceeding south along the east walk we come first to the chapter house, of which the entrance remains—a wide door with a *trumeau*, flanked by windows. Originally this led into a large room about 60 feet deep where the whole convent could meet. On the floor above was the dormitory, a long room continuing the line of the south transept, taking up all the east side of the cloister and extending beyond it. The south walk was flanked along its whole

A curious carving over the door of the north transept representing a Norman bishop, probably from the monument of Herbert de Losinga himself, founder of the abbey and cathedral, who died in 1119. He stands between spiral-fluted columns; the tops of these columns are crude Corinthian capitals, the bottoms dragons' heads. 39

length by the refectory and here a substantial part of the Norman building may still be seen. The wall standing next to the cloister (built in 1175–1200) stands to its full original height, complete with 23 shafted windows. The kitchen would have been at the west end.

The west range, being nearest to the outside world, contained the guests' hall and the parlour, where monks could receive visitors. Parts of the wall adjoining the cloister still exist, with the characteristic interlacing arcade of the late Norman style.

As we have already seen, the layout just described was absolutely standard in Benedictine monasteries and was never varied without compelling reason. Outside the 'claustral unit' the only really important feature was the infirmary, which had its own kitchen and chapel and often its own cloister as well. It was placed near the monks' quarters and there was always easy communication between infirmary and cloister by a passage running under the intervening buildings and often called (as at Norwich) 'the Dark Entry'. At Norwich the infirmary buildings lay to the south.

The Bishop's Palace was kept as remote as possible from the monastery. Here it is on the north side, with its own entrance to the church and its own gateway to the outside world. Some parts of the Norman palace are still visible (a doorway, some windows and an undercroft) but it was remodelled in the middle ages and drastically enlarged in the 19th century, so that its original appearance is hard to reconstruct.

In 1144 a twelve-year-old boy was found dead in a wood on the outskirts of the town and the Jews were accused of murdering him. The boy became a martyr and then, in the eyes of the people, a saint. Miracles began to occur at his grave. His body, after lying in the cemetery was reinterred in a shrine in the cathedral, and the cult of St William of Norwich was launched. It was to be perhaps the abbey's most lucrative single source of revenue for the next 400 years. Bishop Everard, however, seems to have been disillusioned by the conduct of his monks, either over this incident or in general, and soon afterwards resigned his see and went to the Cistercian abbey of Fontenay in France, where we shall meet him again.

The monastery of Norwich was in general on very bad terms with the town, and the high walls with which it surrounded itself were certainly not just for decoration. In August 1272 this antagonism reached a peak of violence when a body of mercenaries hired by the bishop left the abbey and began pillaging the town. The townsmen retaliated, beat them back and set fire to the monastery. Probably

Above, the chapel of St Luke, on the south side of the choir. The strange triple-curve of the wall results from the desire to unite an apsidal chapel opening off the ambulatory with an apse facing due east. The smaller bulge is a staircase.

Right, Norwich from the south-east. The cathedral and cloister are clear enough, but practically all trace of the monastic buildings has disappeared, except for the refectory wall on the south side of the cloister. Note, however, the sham upper wall of the north walk of the cloister and the outline of the Lady Chapel on the turf.

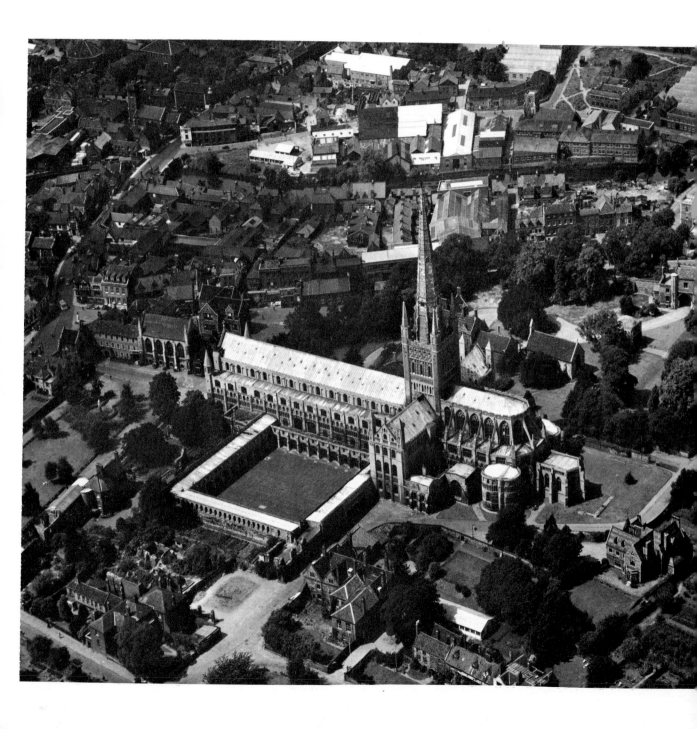

Above, the nave of Norwich, which shows the Norman style at its most monumental. Arcade and gallery are equal in height and make an equal visual impact. In the arcade the supports alternate between main piers (with triple shafts facing into the arch, and twin shafts towards the nave) and subsidiary piers (a shallow curve on the inside and a single shaft reaching only to mid-gallery facing the nave). The clerestory is divided into three, with a central light. The only ornament is a restrained billet moulding on the ground floor and zigzag above. The vault is mid-15th century.

Left, the crossing and choir, looking east. The two lower stages, as well as the crossing piers in the foreground, go back to the first cathedral begun by de Losinga in 1096. The clerestory was built after the old building had been damaged by the fall of the spire in 1362; the intricate vault came last, at the end of the 15th century.

most of the oldest abbey documents perished in the fire; at any rate, from this date onwards the accounts survive in a gratifyingly full state—in all, about 1400 parchment rolls listing every item of income and expenditure. The abbey revenue came from two main sources: offerings and rents. Both were substantial, since the shrine of St William was a famous place of pilgrimage and the abbey estates were extensive. The ways in which it was spent were under the direction of 12 officers, all answerable to the prior: the cellarer, sacrist, chamberlain, precentor, almoner, infirmarer, commoner, pittancer, hostellar, refectorian, gardener and warden of St Paul's Hospital. The sacrist dealt with the upkeep of the fabric, as well as with the embellishment of shrines and altars, repairs of vestments, provision of plate, lanterns, clocks, musical instruments and dozens of other items. He was a busy man and he had six assistants, all monks, though the men employed to do the actual work, including building, would normally be laymen.

Traces of fire are still to be found in one particular spot, which incidentally contains the knottiest architectural mystery in the whole

From the south the full length of Norwich can be appreciated. These extremely long Romanesque naves were peculiar to England. The triple rhythm of the clerestory is easily seen on the exterior; beneath it comes the row of Perpendicular windows inserted to admit more light to the gallery. The tower, with its circular openings, displays more decoration than the rest of the church. To the right rise the tall windows of the later choir.

Left, the north and east cloister walks, the last and first to be built. The east (right in the photograph) was built about 1300. The north side is more than a hundred years later in date and its upper storey is the sham façade. Over all rises the great Norman crossing tower with its spire added in the 15th century after the old one had collapsed.

Opposite, inside the east walk of the cloister, looking south. The door on the left led to the slype, a passage by which the monks could reach the eastern parts of the monastery. The three bays beyond that were originally the entrance to the chapter house, but have long since been walled up.

Only one wall of the refectory still stands, but it is enough to show the scale of the monastic buildings. The view, below, is from inside: the windows, which overlooked the south walk of the old cloister, were blocked when the cloister gained its upper storey.

cathedral. The piers of the nave are all of a uniform composite section, except for one pair—number 5, counting west from the crossing. This is a thick circular pillar with spiral grooving. Why? The mystery deepens when we go back to number 3 on the north side and see, through a hole in the stonework, that this too was originally the same type but has been encased in thicker masonry to make it resemble the others. And on this 'buried' pier are unmistakable signs of fire. The explanation seems to be that originally numbers 1, 3 and 5 were of the circular spiral type (subsidiary piers) alternating with the thicker composite kind (main piers); that after number 5 had been built (in other words, after the pause already mentioned) it was decided to make every pier the same, possibly because the circular type was thought to be too weak; that after a fire (perhaps one recorded in 1170) had damaged them, the first two were encased to strengthen them and number 5 left in its original state. Nevertheless it is only fair to say that this explanation (like all others) is pure conjecture.

The present cloisters replaced those ruined in 1272 over a long period between 1297 and 1430. In the circumstances it is surprising that they are so consistent. Only the changing tracery and the sculptured bosses of the vault betray the lapse of time. Both these features are outstanding. The bosses contain a wealth of fine carving, with scenes from the life of Christ in the north and part of the east walks and from the Apocalypse in the south and west. The tracery includes early Decorated in the east range (c. 1300), beautiful flowing curvilinear in the south (1326 and later) and developed Perpendicular in the north (early 15th). The south walk is perhaps the most interesting of all, since it contains the first signs of the style that was to become Perpendicular, with mullions running straight up into the arch. The designer was William Ramsey, who later worked on St Stephen's Chapel, Westminster, and the chapter house of Old St Paul's, two of the most influential works of the new style.

The cloister at Norwich not only has a most unusual feature—an upper storey—but also one that is unique: one side of it, the north, is only a dummy wall, put there for reasons of symmetry. A building on this side (that is, against the south side of the church) would have prevented light entering the south aisle. The scriptorium of the abbey was probably one of the rooms of the upper storey. The lavatory (in its original meaning of a place for washing) still survives close to the refectory. The monks would wash their hands before coming in to dine. According to a medieval description of Durham, which

could equally well apply to Norwich, 'Next to the conduit door there hung a bell to give warning at 11 o'clock for the monks to come and wash and dine, having the closet and aumbries on either side of the frater door, kept always with sweet and clean towels to dry their hands'. In another part of the cloister are traces of game-boards cut into the stone benches by novices.

In 1362 the spire collapsed, crushing the upper part of the choir. The clerestory was then rebuilt higher than its Norman predecessor. The present choir is thus a confusing mixture of styles, for the Norman arcade was covered with a filigree of Perpendicular tracery at the end of the 15th century while the old triforium remains, above which is the new clerestory; the whole is crowned by a rich lierne vault dating from 1480–90.

The only other major addition to the cathedral's fabric was the vault of the nave, similar to that of the choir but slightly earlier (1450–70). Both are as rich in sculptured bosses as the cloisters.

The Norwich choir stalls, below left, are among the most complete in England, and contain a wealth of lively and amusing carving. This part of the church was reserved for the monks, and was divided from the laymen's part —the west bays of the nave—by a stone pulpitum where the modern organ stands.

Right, The Chapel of Carnary College, founded by Bishop Salmon in 1316 and still used by the school. It has a spacious undercroft, used in the middle ages as a charnel house.

Below, St Ethelbert's Gate, built by Bishop Salmon in 1316, with money paid by the town of Norwich as a fine after the riots of 1272. Its most striking feature is the flintwork at the top. Such pattern-making in flint was very much an East Anglian speciality.

47

Norwich is also fortunate in its choir stalls of roughly the same date (in fact, from 1420 to 1480). In monastic times they would have occupied the crossing and the first few bays of the nave, a stone pulpitum or screen closing them off from the rest of the cathedral, which was open to the laity. Each stall has a traceried front and canopied back and the seats are those known as misericords (*misericordia* is Latin for pity); they have a projection on their outer edge so that when tipped up they provide some support for the monk in a half-standing position. The underside of the seats are carved with lively, often secular and sometimes violently anti-clerical, subjects. The introduction of comfortable stalls with misericords seems to have come fairly late, and these mitigated at least to some extent the austerities of the monk's life. An account of Cluniac customs written about 1080 (probably for an abbot of Reichenau) gives a rather touching description of the all-too-human weakness that might overcome a monk during the long night services. One of the brethren went round the choir with a lantern, 'and if he thought that anyone were asleep he held it up to his face; if he turned out to be awake he bowed reverently; if he were really asleep he brought the lantern close to his eyes to waken him'.

The end of the monastery of Norwich is a depressing story. The compromise between secular and religious roles, the divided authority, the running fight between abbey and town, all combined to prevent it achieving real greatness. It played a more glorious role as a cathedral than it did as an abbey. When Bishop Goldwell visited the monks officially in 1492 he found that the prior was negligent; that the gates were never shut and that the wives of the abbey servants spent the night there; that valuables had been sold; that one monk, Father Denys, held five of the twelve offices; and that the monks wasted much of their time talking to lay people, including women of doubtful reputation. Some twenty years later things seem to have been just as easy-going. When Bishop Nykke held a visitation in 1514 the prior did not bother to appear and made no apology for his absence; the buildings were dilapidated; women went in and out freely; and sheep were grazing in the cloister.

Such was the state of affairs on the eve of the Dissolution, which came in 1538. The monastic buildings were then left to decay or were used as quarries for stone, sometimes for the cathedral, which in spite of some narrow escapes has survived intact until the present day. But monasticism in England disappeared for 300 years.

The great cathedral abbey of Norwich still dominates the city with its lofty central spire. The bishopric was transferred here by the Normans from the small East Anglian town of Thetford, and as was common with such foundations it served a dual purpose—as the bishop's cathedral and as a Benedictine abbey-church. This view from the east shows the apse with its three chapels (the central one modern) and tall clerestory windows of the Decorated period. Like so many English churches, Norwich is a composite of all the medieval styles, so that the final result seems not so much designed by architects as evolved by history itself.

CHAPTER 2

MONT ST MICHEL:
THE BENEDICTINES IN FRANCE

If Norwich shows the Benedictines immersed in the affairs of the world, Mont St Michel shows them, at least to begin with, at the opposite extreme. Few places in medieval France were so inaccessible, so inhospitable and so cut off from the outside world.

The earliest monks at Mont St Michel are said to have been two hermits, who took possession of the main island off the coast of Brittany and the smaller island of Tombelaine, a mile or so to the north. They could be reached only at low tide, and the flowing sea was so treacherous that even when they became popular places of pilgrimage it was common enough for people to be drowned. A regular monastery was founded in the eighth century and there are picturesque legends connected with it. Aubert, Bishop of Avranches, the nearest big town, is said to have had a series of dreams in which St Michael appeared to him and ordered him to found a monastery on the Mount. The bishop delayed longer than the archangel thought reasonable and on his third visit he touched the bishop on the head as a reminder. The skull, with a neat hole in the top, used to be shown to visitors as proof. This story in fact provides an unnecessary explanation, for the dedication of hill-top sites to St Michael was an ancient custom that was common all over Europe. The most famous example (which was certainly known to the founders of Mont St Michel) was Monte Gargano in Apulia.

The Mount became a refuge for the people of the surrounding countryside during the devastations of the Norsemen. These refugees were probably the original inhabitants of the town that still clusters round its base. Normandy eventually came entirely under Norman control, and it was the grandson of the first duke, Richard 50 the Fearless, who took the step that really inaugurates the history

ERVNT:AD MON TE MICHAELIS   ET HIC:TRANSI

'Here Duke William and his army came to Michael's mount'; a detail from the Bayeux Tapestry, probably made about 1080. Simplified as this representation is, it does show very clearly how the middle of the church rests on the rock while the two ends are held up by supports.

of Mont St Michel as we know it. In 966 he ejected the monks then in possession on the ground of laxness and replaced them by regular Benedictines from St Wadrille and Jumièges, two of the leading monasteries in Normandy. The earliest part of the abbey dates from this time or soon after. This is the chapel of *Notre Dame sous Terre*, underneath the nave of the present church (or rather underneath the platform where the western bays of the nave used to be)—a simple chamber of four bays, the roof supported on a large square pier.

In 1017 Richard II of Normandy was married to Judith of Brittany at Mont St Michel, chosen because it was exactly on the border of the two dukedoms. The wedding seems to have brought the Mount into the limelight and it became the recipient of some substantial patronage. Under the leadership of Richard's adviser, William of Volpiano, the influence of Cluny was now paramount in Normandy. It was the signal for a decisive enlargement of the church and monastery.

Mont St Michel has always been unlike any other monastery in the world. Built as it was on the sides of a precipitous rock, there was no question of its ever following the traditional pattern. Once that pattern has been grasped, however, it is interesting to see how far the monks of Mont St Michel fitted its component parts together in a new way. The elements of the Benedictine plan, instead of being laid out side by side, are literally piled on top of one another.

The church, built on the highest part of the rock, was begun soon

Opposite, *the* Salle de l'Aquilon, *one of the earliest parts of the monastic buildings at Mont St Michel. In the 11th century it was a well-lit room, covered by a wooden ceiling, where the monks could walk and congregate.*   51

after 1017, and finished about a hundred years later. It consisted of choir, transepts and nave, but only the middle part (the crossing and the first four bays of the nave) could be built on the solid rock. For the rest, large substructures had to be erected. The choir rested on a high crypt (both choir and crypt collapsed in 1421 and were replaced by the present building; the original choir was probably only two bays long, with the same elevation as the nave, ending in an apse); the transepts on massive rooms serving as chapels; and the western part of the nave on the old Carolingian church, which henceforth became *sous terre*.

The approach to the church was much the same as it is now. A steep path, often breaking into steps, led from a point due east of the choir all the way past the south side of the church (with one twist) and finished at the west end, where there were two towers and a porch or narthex. The monks' quarters, which were necessarily cramped, were on the north side, where they had a *promenoir* (a sort of closed-in cloister), a refectory and kitchen—all at crypt level—and a dormitory, infirmary and work-room on the level of the church.

The first part of all to be built, however, was a room underneath the *promenoir* called the *Salle de l'Aquilon*. It was formerly lit from the north but the windows were later blocked by the group of buildings known as the *Merveille*, giving it a cellar-like appearance. The *promenoir* acted as the monastery's cloister until the present one was built at the top of the *Merveille* (which we shall discuss shortly). It is a long room, now vaulted, but in the 11th century probably covered by a wooden ceiling.

The church itself has been so rebuilt and restored that its original appearance is not so easy to recapture. The choir will be described later; the tower and the crossing had to be rebuilt in 1900; and the three western bays of the nave were pulled down in 1776 because of fear of collapse. The interior nave elevation, however, remains, and it is in the stern uncompromising style familiar to any student of the Norman cathedrals of England: an arcade of round arches, a triforium subdivided into three, and a clerestory. Long wall shafts rise from the floor to the middle of the clerestory, where they supported the beams of the old timber roof.

In 1203 there was a disastrous fire on the north side, during which some houses belonging to the abbey were set ablaze by a Breton marauder. The abbot, Jourdain, took the opportunity to expand the monastic buildings on a large scale. The result is the block known as the *Merveille*, a practically self-contained unit of three floors

Three plans of Mont St Michel showing, from left to right, the level of the sub-structures; the level of the crypt des gros piliers; *and the level of the church.*

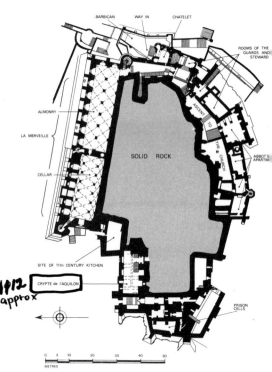

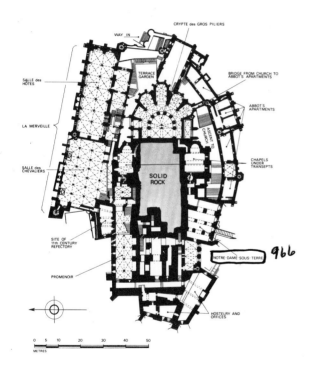

CRYPTE des GROS PILIERS

WAY IN

TERRACE
GARDEN

BRIDGE FROM CHURCH TO
ABBOT'S APARTMENTS

SALLE des
HÔTES

ABBOT'S
APARTMENTS

LA MERVEILLE

ASCENT TO CHURCH

SALLE des
CHEVALIERS

SOLID
ROCK

CHAPELS
UNDER
TRANSEPTS

SITE OF
11th CENTURY
REFECTORY

966

NOTRE DAME SOUS TERRE

PROMENOIR

HOSTELRY AND
OFFICES

0 5 10   20   30   40   50
METRES

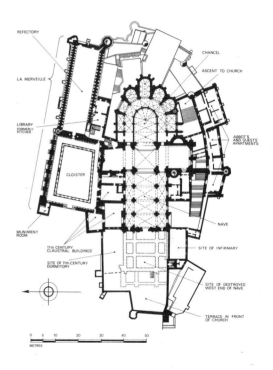

REFECTORY

CHANCEL

LA MERVEILLE

ASCENT TO CHURCH

LIBRARY
FORMERLY
KITCHEN

ABBOT'S
AND GUESTS'
APARTMENTS

CLOISTER

NAVE

MUNIMENT
ROOM

11th CENTURY
CLAUSTRAL BUILDINGS

SITE OF INFIRMARY

SITE OF 11th CENTURY
DORMITORY

SITE OF DESTROYED
WEST END OF NAVE

TERRACE IN FRONT
OF CHURCH

0 5 10   20   30   40   50
METRES

each divided into two large halls and comprising as a whole one of the most perfect examples of early 13th-century domestic architecture anywhere in Europe. The story of its building is not quite as simple as it appears at first sight. In the first place, there was something there before: the two lowest rooms, known as the cellar and the almonry, seem in part to date from before 1203. Secondly, it is at least possible that the intention was to build only half of the present block, the western half, and that the decision to enlarge it to its present area was taken at some stage when operations had already begun.

The almonry is a long groin-vaulted room supported in the middle by a row of columns, lit, as are all the rooms of the *Merveille*, by windows on the north side. Next to it, on the same level, is the cellar, a wider room with a double row of square piers.

When we move up to the next floor we are unmistakably in the early 13th century. The rooms have greater spaciousness and elegance, though it may easily be seen (by referring to the plan) that their supports stand exactly on those below—the *Salle des Hôtes* over the almonry and the *Salle des Chevaliers* over the cellar. These two rooms acquired their names relatively recently and their original function is still a matter of some disagreement. The whole of the *Merveille* has suffered many alterations in its long history, making it difficult to assign the rooms to their first monastic use. The *Salle des Hôtes* has graceful quadripartite rib vaults with small bosses. A small chapel opens off it, from which one can reach the crypt of the church and a little terrace garden to the east. This implies a certain degree of comfort, even of luxury, and lends colour to the suggestion that this is where the abbot entertained his guests. Perhaps it was also his Hall of Justice.

The *Salle des Chevaliers*, the other room on this floor, is wider and grander—wider in fact than the room underneath, for it has three rows of columns instead of two, the southernmost one resting on the solid rock. The name dates from the 15th century. (Louis XI founded the military Order of St Michael in 1469, and originally intended that its ceremonies should be held here, the archangel's most famous sanctuary in France. But as might have been foreseen, it was too far away from Paris and too inconvenient for the noble recipients of the honour, so a chapel of St Michael was built near the Palais Royal in the capital.) Various suggestions have been made about the original purpose of the *Salle des Chevaliers*; possibly it was the dormitory, possibly the scriptorium, for Mont St Michel

Above, the south side of the nave. The style is typical of Norman Romanesque, which also became standard in England after the Conquest. The original roof would have been flat and of wood.

Above right, the Salle des Hôtes. *This long 13th-century hall, whose original use is uncertain, stands directly underneath the refectory. Signs of damage to the walls and vaults show the treatment it received as a fortress and a prison.*

Above, the almonry, one of the rooms at the lowest level of the Merveille. Though pre-dating the rest by a few years, its simple details and general solidity are dictated mainly by its function and the fact that it had to support two storeys above it.

was by this date becoming famous as a literary centre. With its wide, simple proportions and fine detail, this is perhaps the most imposing room in the whole abbey.

On the roof itself of their vertical monastery the monks built their refectory and cloister. The refectory (finished in about 1225) is a light airy room which, because it is at the top of the whole structure, needed no internal supports for a load-bearing roof. The most interesting feature is provided by the windows, over thirty narrow lancets on the north and nearly as many on the south, so that the interior is brightly lit; but they are all placed inside an arcade of deep niches so that from the door one cannot see them at all. On the north side is the pulpit from which one of the brethren read aloud at meals. The kitchen opened off the refectory on the south side (tucked in between the *Merveille* and the church) but was later converted into a library.

If we leave the refectory by the west door we come to the cloister, which stands on top of the *Salle des Chevaliers* and spreads out into an irregular quadrilateral to take in as much spare space as possible. From its windows one can look out far across the rocks and sands to Tombelaine. Or turning inward one is faced by the graceful

double arcade of the cloister walks, two overlapping rows of pointed arches, which creates a sort of syncopated rhythm of alternating arch and shaft as one moves along it. The spandrels are decorated with naturalistic foliage carving.

The cloister was the last work of the *Merveille* but it was not the end of the monks' ambitions. They intended to extend their monastery by building another three-storey block to the west, as is testified by the doorways still remaining at various levels. On the west side of the cloister is the traditional tripartite entrance to a chapter house, almost in its traditional place, but opening on to empty air. Looking down from this lofty spot one gains a forcible impression of the boldness and imagination of these 13th-century builders. At the extreme outer edge of the cloister is the muniment room where the charters and monastic records were kept.

Historically we have now reached the middle of the 13th century. At this time Mont St Michel was at the peak of its greatness. It had been led by a series of capable and energetic abbots: Maynard I, the first Benedictine abbot; Roger I, chaplain to William the Conqueror, who retired to England and died there; Bernard the Venerable, who finished the Romanesque church; Robert de Torigni, 'valued by kings, revered by queens, loved by all', who ruled Mont St Michel for over thirty years (1154–86) and greatly increased its

Opposite, the Salle des Chevaliers, *so-called because the Knights of St Michael were once supposed to have held meetings there. This is the grandest room at Mont St Michel, and shows the 13th century at its most splendid.*

Left, the refectory, looking west. The central door opens into the cloister; those to the left led originally to the kitchen. On the extreme right is part of the stair to the reader's pulpit.

Above, the crypte des gros piliers; *these thick pillars support the whole east end of the church. Built in the mid-15th century, they are almost entirely without decoration (note the absence of capitals) but have a certain elegance, which distinguishes them from equally massive Romanesque work.*

Opposite, the cloister, on the roof of the Merveille. *The foliage carving on the upper parts, the intriguing alternation of the double arcade and the wide views of sea and sky must have made this a spot of particular charm.*

Left, a view down into the choir. New to Mont St Michel were the crisp linear mouldings of the arcade and the finely carved double tracery of the triforium. Each of the piers rests on one of the big pillars of the crypt.

59

reputation for learning (it was under him that the famous Cartulary, the chief source for the abbey's history, was compiled); Jourdain, who began the *Merveille*; Raoul, who completed it; Tustin, the first abbot of the Mount to be made a bishop.

This last fact is significant, for the secular importance of Mont St Michel now begins to rival the religious. As France grew into a nation, absorbing the old duchy of Normandy, the Mount, strategically placed as it was, could not help assuming the role of a fortress. Louis IX (St Louis) visited it in 1256 and made grants towards its upkeep and defence. At the end of the century a regular garrison was established. The Hundred Years War against England was on the point of breaking out and Mont St Michel was in the front line. There is unfortunately no space to describe the fortifications, prominent and historically interesting as they are. Indeed the 14th century is largely a chronicle of sieges and raids.

In 1421 the old crypt collapsed, bringing down the choir above it. The war was still on and no repairs were made for thirty years. When work did begin in 1452 it progressed slowly and was not finished until 1521. It is therefore one of the last major works of French Gothic and for this reason alone is of great interest. Not surprisingly, it is the most highly decorated part of Mont St Michel, though even so it was not as lavish as many other examples of the Flamboyant style. The crypt, indeed, is distinctly sober. It rests on massive round piers without capitals, the ribs dying into the stone. Upstairs in the choir proper there is far more enrichment—clusters of thin shafts and delicate flame-like tracery in the windows. On the exterior, with its filigree of stone between the flying buttresses, the effect is even more striking. Yet some features, such as the square panels in the triforium and the high bases to the shafts, are reminiscent of the Perpendicular style of contemporary England.

In monastic times the choir, as at Norwich, would have extended beyond the crossing and into the nave. The crossing was surmounted by a tower, which was partly of wood and which burned down in 1564. It was replaced by one of stone and later still by the one now to be seen there.

The remainder of Mont St Michel's history is one of decline. In 1594 it played a part in the religious wars, when about 80 Huguenots were lured inside by a trick and murdered. In 1622 the resident monks, accused like their brethren of the 10th century of laxness, were replaced by Benedictines of the Congregation of St Maur. This had been founded only a few years before as a strict order

Above, an air-view of Mont St Michel from the south-west. The whole group is dominated by the tower and spire (restored in 1900). In front of this is the truncated nave with its makeshift 18th-century façade. Signs of collapse and modern buttressing are evident at the corner nearest the camera.

dedicated to scholarship and teaching. Their schools, both for rich and poor, became famous. They were organised under a 'superior general' and part of their training consisted of a five-year course in philosophy and theology; in this respect they were similar to the Jesuits, but they were real monks and their rule was strictly Benedictine. To Mont St Michel they evidently brought a new religious vitality but were hampered by the condition of the place and their lack of funds to repair it. During the next fifty years the north transept was walled off as unsafe; the cloister pavement boarded over; the refectory divided horizontally by the insertion of a new floor, the top part being used as a granary; party walls were built in the *Salle des Hôtes* and the *Salle des Chevaliers*; and fireplaces were installed in several of the rooms.

In 1769 the whole abbey was in such bad repair that the abbot Etienne de Bienne, Archbishop of Toulouse, resigned his abbacy to the king. Under Louis XVI some work was carried out (for example, the new west front) but the Revolution soon cut short any further plans. With the Terror the monastic life of Mont St Michel—and of France—came to a stop. The monks were driven out, the property sold, and the buildings turned into a prison. Unhappily it proved so

The *'lace stair'* (escalier de dentelle) *running up one of the flying buttresses of the choir; the stairway lies between the two diagonal rails with their curvilinear tracery.*

Left, a view from the tower, looking east. Below the abbey buildings lies the picturesque village street, and at the edge of the sea a bastion of the 15th-century ramparts.

Right, the island of Mont St Michel from the air. First chosen as a place of refuge by hermits in the dark ages, the rock was taken over by Benedictine monks in the 10th century. Its isolation and almost impregnable position made it at the same time a place of pilgrimage and a fortress. A ring of ramparts encircles its base; higher up, below the church, can be seen the massive walls and barbican of the monastic defences; while on the other side, slightly to the right, rises the three-storey 13th-century building known as the Merveille.

well suited to this purpose that it so remained, under Napoleon and the restored Bourbons, until 1863. The damage done during these years was extensive and in some ways irreparable. Most of the accessible sculpture was destroyed, holes were hacked in the stone-work and the fabric was neglected until it was little more than a sordid ruin. After 1874 it was classed as a *monument historique* and the restoration it underwent thereafter was in some respects hardly less ruthless than the previous vandalism. Viollet-le-Duc rebuilt the battlements and defensive bastions, and covered the cloister-walks with his favourite polychrome tiles. But in recent years antiquarian taste has changed and this 'restoration' has been 'unrestored' again. Mont St Michel stands now amid the trappings of the tourist industry, almost as gaunt and comfortless as it was six hundred years ago.

CHAPTER 3

FONTENAY:
ST BERNARD AND THE CISTERCIANS

The Cistercian Order was a movement within Benedictine monasticism aimed at a return to the simplicity of the original Rule. In this it resembled Cluny, but the men who led it had the lessons (and as they saw it, the mistakes) of Cluny before them and determined to reach their goal by another road. They realised that power, influence and wealth would inevitably be barriers on this road, however worthy they might be in other respects. The remedy, therefore, was to go back to poverty and austerity, to leave the centres of population, to perform hard manual work as St Benedict had laid down and to concentrate on the essentials of the religious life and the path to salvation. Hence their monasteries were built in remote districts and are often well preserved. Indeed, it is a picture of a typical Cistercian abbey that the words 'medieval monastery' conjure up in the mind.

The order began in a small way. In 1098 Robert, Abbot of Molesme, a house with Cluniac affiliations, obtained permission from the Archbishop of Lyons to found a new house in which these new reforms could be put into practice. With twenty companions he retired to the solitude of Cîteaux, in Burgundy, where he established an independent community. At first there was trouble with Molesme and Robert had to return after a year, but the rest of the monks remained. In 1100 the pope exempted them from outside interference and the Cistercian Order was born. (The name comes from *Cistercium*, the Latin form of Cîteaux.)

Their constitution was based on the Benedictine Rule, but they took certain steps to distinguish themselves from the previous Benedictines. They changed their black habit to white (at the personal suggestion of the Virgin Mary, it was said) and they

organised themselves to be as far as possible self-supporting. Besides the monks were the so-called *conversi* or lay brothers, men who took the same vows but who were illiterate and could therefore never be ordained (as the monks increasingly were) or take part in the choir services. They were forbidden to aspire to become full monks and even to learn to read (this was supposed to prevent envy and ambition), but had to accept their position as lay brothers for the rest of their lives. For their own services, which were held in the nave of the church, they recited a liturgy that they learnt by heart. As time went on, much of the farm work and administration was taken over by the lay brothers, who usually outnumbered the monks.

Like St Benedict, the first Cistercians did not see themselves as founding a new order; but their vigour, sincerity and achievements made it inevitable that they should become examples to others. The second and third abbots of Cîteaux were both members of the original party from Molesme—Alberic, who died in 1109, and Stephen Harding, an Englishman, a scholar and an able administrator. But in 1112 they were joined by a man who was perhaps the greatest genius the monastic movement ever produced, and from that moment the order bore the unmistakable impress of his personality.

St Bernard was 22 when he presented himself at Cîteaux and begged admission to the order. He came from one of the oldest and noblest families of Burgundy and had already shown exceptional

Above, Fontenay from the west. Its secluded valley is typical of Cistercian sites. In this view the small round building in the foreground is the dovecote; the west front of the church is on the left and the forge on the extreme right.

Opposite, the interior of the church looking east. Fontenay epitomises the Cistercian ideal and contains all the standard features of their churches—the arcade of unmoulded pointed arches, pointed barrel vault, clerestory (no gallery), straight-ended chancel and complete absence of ornament.

ability as a scholar. He was also, evidently, a natural leader; when he came to Cîteaux thirty other young noblemen came with him. And two years later Abbot Stephen gave him the responsibility of founding a daughter-house at Clairvaux, a name that from then on was inseparably joined with his own.

Clairvaux was the third daughter-house of Cîteaux. As the numbers grew many more followed, and then daughters of those daughters, a process that led to an important development in the Cistercian constitution. It was determined to hold the Cistercian family together in unity, but instead of being under the absolute rule of one superior, as at Cluny, it was to be an equal partnership. Each abbey governed itself but was subject to inspection by the abbot of the founding mother-house. 'Visits' by the abbots were a regular feature of Cistercian life, taking place once a year. Even more important was the annual 'chapter' of the whole order, when all the abbots met for discussion, decision and exchange of views. These 'general chapters' were held every year from 1119 until 1411. It was a system that did in fact succeed in carrying out the work it was meant to do—that is, to encourage the best and weed out the corrupt, and the Cistercian record during these years is as exemplary as that of any human institution can hope to be.

St Bernard was a crusader and, admittedly, in many ways a fanatic. But his case against the worldliness of the Cluniacs had reason as well as fervour on its side, and the impact was tremendous:

'I say nothing about the enormous height of your churches, their unnecessary length and breadth, the elaborate carving and painting which catches the worshipper's eye and distracts his attention, and which seems to me a sort of revival of ancient Jewish rites. Let all this pass—say that it is done to the glory of God. But, as a monk, I ask this of my brother monks: Tell me, you "poor men", if poor you really are, what is all this gold doing in your sanctuary? The bishops may have an excuse; *they* have to deal with the stupid as well as the wise, they cannot excite the devotion of ordinary people by spiritual things and are forced to do it by decoration and splendour. But *we*, who have cut ourselves off from the world, who have renounced its wealth and beauty for Christ's sake, who have counted everything pleasant to the senses as nothing but dung—whose devotion, pray, do we excite by such things?'

It is the desire of gain, he goes on to say, that makes the monas-

Above, a view across the nave from one aisle into the other, showing how each aisle bay is vaulted transversely. This supports the high vault and divides the aisle into a series of spaces.

Lying low in its moist valley, the Cistercian abbey of Fontenay (opposite) speaks the harsh, austere language of St Bernard, the great reformer who led monasticism back to its first ideals. Here the church, seen from the east, is on the right. To the left is the chapter house (originally larger) and part of the dormitory range. Over the gable is the belfry—the modest Cistercian substitute for a bell-tower. 67

teries stoop to these devices; the gaudier the image, the greater the pilgrim's offering. 'Money is expended that it may give increase', for at the sight of these 'costly yet marvellous vanities men are more inspired to offer gifts than to pray.' So the churches are filled with golden images, chandeliers 'like cart-wheels' studded with jewels and candelabra of bronze. 'The Church clothes her stones with gold and leaves her sons naked; the rich man's eye is fed at the expense of the poor; the curious find delight, the needy find no relief.'

Only by quoting St Bernard at some length is it possible to convey the passion behind his indictment, and only in these terms does the cool, practical, devoted austerity of Cistercian architecture make its full effect. These churches are plain, are bare, are in some respects less interesting than the churches that he was attacking, and to appreciate their merits requires something more than a mere aesthetic reaction, no matter how cultivated. For the effect of St Bernard's teaching was to banish all 'art' in the sense of non-structural ornament. He makes bitter fun of Romanesque capitals such as those illustrated in the Introduction—the centaurs, tigers, knights fighting, beasts who are part-serpent, part-horse, part-goat—which he calls ridiculous monsters. And who needs mosaic pavements, where 'the face of some saint is ground under the heel

Above, the transept, looking north. On the right is the entrance to the chancel and beyond it two of the flanking chapels.

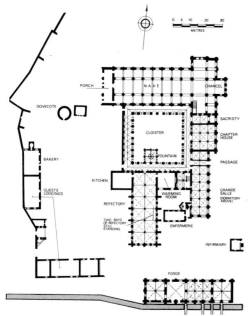

Left, a plan of Fontenay abbey.

The west front, above, still has its original windows but has lost its porch. A row of brackets mark its roof-line; it probably had a central door flanked by large windows, with pairs of smaller windows on each side.

Centre, two views of the cloister, the upper looking from one of the lavatorium arches towards the west part of the nave; the lower looking north-east and showing the north transept where it adjoins the dormitory. Above the dormitory gable is the bell-turret, with two bells, one above the other—the Cistercian substitute for the high towers of the Cluniacs. 69

of every passer by'? Yet for the flowering of another kind of art—
that of structure, of pure form and the relation of simple masses—
St Bernard's ideals offered abundant opportunity.

The Cistercians increased with a rapidity that must have astonished
even themselves. Clairvaux alone, in the lifetime of St Bernard,
founded 68 new monasteries. When he died in 1153 the whole
order comprised 300 abbeys and was still growing. To generalise
about them is comparatively easy because they are highly stan-
dardised. Churches are severe, undecorated and strongly built;
they had no crypts, no towers and square east ends. (A decree of
the General Chapter of 1124 forbade sculptural embellishments as
well as illuminations in manuscripts; another in 1157 banned towers,
and another in 1182, stained glass.) Conventual buildings have the
same qualities: the lower storeys were usually vaulted; the refectory,
for some reason, was placed at right angles to the south wall of the
cloister instead of lying along it; and the west range was given over
to the lay brothers, who worshipped in the nave of the church and
had a door of their own. The public was not admitted. Provision for
guests was less lavish than in the older monasteries but it was still
part of the Rule. Much of the building was carried out by the brethren
themselves—a fact that probably gave rise to the old myth that all
medieval churches were built by monks. The master-masons were,
in fact, usually members of the order (one of them was St Bernard's
brother Gérard). The style they evolved and made standard was
essentially Burgundian Romanesque reduced to its most practical
form and embodying certain progressive engineering features that
were to become characteristic of Gothic, in particular the pointed
arch. It has been christened 'Cistercian half-Gothic'.

Nearly everything at both Cîteaux and Clairvaux was destroyed
during the Revolution; Fontenay is therefore the oldest Cistercian
abbey now standing in France. It was founded from Clairvaux in
1118 and its first abbot was a relative of St Bernard. The original
settlement was half a mile from its present position, but it proved too
cramped; in 1130 the monks moved down the valley. It was an ideal
place for a Cistercian foundation: uninhabited, but with cultivable
land near by and a stream for drinking water and drainage. (The
site was given to them by yet another of St Bernard's relations; one
is tempted to speculate about the early success of this austere order
had St Bernard been less well connected.) Their first church seems to
have been small and temporary but in 1139, as we have already seen,
70 Bishop Everard of Norwich came to Fontenay after retiring from

*Below, the chapter house, originally a perfect
square, but the three eastern bays were
demolished and their arches blocked and pierced
with windows (on the right), probably in the
15th century.*

*The cloister (top right) has the same austere
virtues as the church. A heavy barrel vault rests
on square piers, the spaces between being filled
by solid lunettes on coupled columns. This is the
south walk, which in the middle opened, right,
into the* lavatorium *or wash-place and, left, into
the refectory. Neither now survives.*

Bottom right, the Grande Salle, *which resembles
the chapter house, but is sturdier and the details
are less elegant. Its original use is unknown,
and may have varied according to the needs of
the community.*

his troubled diocese in England. He was a rich man, and he subsidised the building of the new church to such an extent that by 1147 it was ready for consecration. Everard himself did not live with the monks. He built himself a comfortable house outside the walls, but he was buried in the choir and his tombstone can still be seen there. The monastic buildings were going forward at about the same time; at least it is fairly certain that they were finished by 1175.

Fontenay, grey, bare, without emphases or striking features, is not an abbey that makes an overwhelming first impression. Nor was it meant to. Lying low in the valley (damp has been a hazard to the architecture ever since it was built) it huddles against the landscape without a single unnecessary gesture. The church itself is even more bleak than it was originally, for its west front lacks its original long porch or narthex, which was a usual Cistercian feature. But the interior is a superb embodiment of the founder's ideals. The lines are stark and clear—a short, straight-ended chancel, transepts each with two straight-ended chapels, nave and aisles. The nave, with its arcade of unmoulded pointed arches, is covered by a pointed tunnel vault with transverse arches resting on wall shafts. The aisles have *transverse* tunnel vaults (that is, the vaults run at right angles to the nave—a series of separate vaults instead of one long one), an economical device that provides buttressing for the high vault of the nave. The effect is to make each bay of the aisles into a self-contained unit, and this was intended. The Cistercians tried to avoid saying more than one Mass a day at any altar; they therefore used the aisle bays as chapels. There is no triforium and no clerestory. The only real enrichment permitted is on the capitals in the aisles, which have a simple interlace pattern.

The cloister is a simple composition of repeated elements: square bays, wide subdivided arches, square piers and coupled colonnettes. Here the capitals are allowed a chaste suggestion of a leaf shape. Walking along its east walk, starting from the church, one comes first to a recess that housed the monastic book cupboard, then to the entrance to the chapter house, a large room originally of nine square bays (the three easternmost ones were demolished, possibly after a fire in 1490) and rib-vaulted, an indication of a slightly later period than that of the church. It opens off the cloister by the usual triple opening (two windows and a door) and is rather a part of the cloister than a separate enclosed space.

After the chapter house, still going south, comes a passage leading to the garden and then a long room vaulted like the chapter

house. and with bays exactly similar in size, now called the *Grande Salle*. This appears to have been a common room or parlour for the monks or else it was used for study. On the upper floor of this whole range was the dormitory, which now has a fine 15th-century timber roof. The latrines were at the south end, close to the river.

Turning west we pass the 'warming room', which still has two 12th-century chimneys, and another room, which may have been the scriptorium. Then came the refectory, a long and obviously very fine hall built later than the rest of the abbey (in the 13th century; it replaced a smaller one), but mostly demolished. It was divided in two by an arcade, rib-vaulted and with a very beautiful interior elevation of alternating single and triple shafts. Two bays of it survive, built into the end wall of the *enfermerie* (which we shall describe later). In front of the refectory entrance, projecting in a square of four bays into the cloister garth, was the *lavatorium*.

The *enfermerie*, a euphemism for prison, is a 16th-century building, which now joins the end of the dormitory wing to the ruins of the refectory. The abbots, like other feudal lords, were also magistrates. They punished, in some cases hanged, malefactors. A decree of the General Chapter of 1229 laid down that every Cistercian abbey was to be provided with a prison. The one at Fontenay has a pleasant Renaissance doorway bearing the date 1547.

Above, the restored south end of the dormitory wing; the ground floor is occupied by the Grande Salle. *On the left is the later prison (enfermerie), ending (extreme left) with the re-used section of the refectory wall.*

Above left, the forge. It was built at the beginning of the 13th century for use by the lay brothers as a smithy and metalwork shop. Millwheels on the far side were turned by the river.

Right, inside the forge. The furnaces in this photograph are fairly late, and have in fact been partly cleared away during the recent restoration. However, they do demonstrate that the forge was, and always had been, an industrial building.

The other buildings at Fontenay, mostly to the south and west of the main group, may be described more briefly. Chief among them is the 13th-century forge. According to St Bernard, a monastery should provide everything it needed from its own resources; workshops were therefore an integral part of all Cistercian foundations. The forge at Fontenay is one of the largest and best preserved. It is a large building of two floors, each containing four vaulted rooms, and was built on the river bank to make use of the hydraulic power. Here were made all the tools and implements needed by the abbey and probably by much of the surrounding countryside. There are still traces of the furnaces and water-wheels. Even so, it is still something of an effort to see this as an industrial building, so mesmerised are we into thinking of the paraphernalia of the Gothic style—piers, capitals, shafts and rib vaults—as exclusively 'religious': a distinction and a way of thinking about architecture that were totally foreign to the middle ages.

There was a host of other buildings at Fontenay, mostly connected with the lodging of guests and the working of the estate, which have largely disappeared or been radically altered. The dovecote, however, of the 14th or early 15th century, remains in a prominent position near the west front, adding a touch of charm to its grey surroundings.

In its heyday Fontenay was a place of renown. The title of *Abbaye Royale* was given to it by St Louis. Several 'little Fontenays' were also founded when the numbers threatened to outgrow the accommodation. In the early 14th century there were 300 monks and lay brethren and large estates accumulated by gift and legacy. In the 15th, however, it entered a period of decline. It was sacked and burnt several times during the Hundred Years War, the dormitory being completely gutted in 1459. By now the Cistercian *élan* had died down. In 1745 the Refectory had to be largely pulled down because it was dangerous, only the two bays mentioned remaining.

During the Revolution the abbey was suppressed and the buildings sold. It became a paper-works. New factories were put up but the old fabric was not too badly damaged. When in 1906 it was taken over by the state, it was found that by removing the later work and carrying out certain minimal repairs the original appearance could to a large extent be restored. Today it is a place of repose and mellow peace—rather too much so perhaps. It is hard to believe that the spirit of St Bernard looks down with approval at the neat lawns, the ornamental fountains and the splashes of colour in the flower-beds.

CHAPTER 4

FOUNTAINS:
THE CISTERCIANS IN ENGLAND

The history of Fountains is documented in great detail from the time of its foundation from the near-by Benedictine abbey of St Mary's, York, to the day it was dissolved four centuries later. For its beginnings we have the eye-witness account of one Serlo:

'When the monks left the monastery of York,' he recalled, 'I myself was present. I had known their names and faces from my boyhood, I was born in their country, and was brought up amongst them, and to several of them I was related by ties of blood. And although I am, as you can see, far advanced in years, I am very grateful to my old age that my memory remains unimpaired, and particularly retentive of those things committed to it in early years. Such things, therefore, relating to the origins of the Monastery of Fountains, which I personally witnessed or have gathered from the credible report of my elders, I will now relate.'

Their reason for leaving York was the simple desire to live more strictly according to the Rule. The decision to join the Cistercians (prompted no doubt by the foundation of Rievaulx the year before) only came after two years of severe privations. Fountains in the 1130s was not the pleasant, cultivated spot that we now see, but 'a place remote from all the world, uninhabited, thick set with thorns, lying between the slopes of mountains and among jutting rocks—fit rather, it seemed, to be the lair of wild beasts than the home of human beings'. They even considered emigrating *en masse* to Burgundy. But a monk from Clairvaux, called Geoffrey, was sent over, instructed them in the rules of the order and presumably also in the building of the monastery. The tide was now turning. Gifts

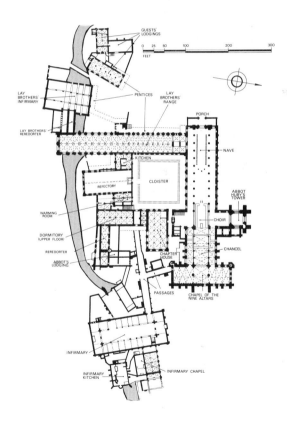

A plan of Fountains abbey.

75

Above, the south side of the nave, a fine example of the severe yet technically very progressive 'Cistercian half-Gothic' of the later 12th century. The sturdy round piers are a superb expression of strength, only slightly marred by the shafts attached to them on the aisle side.

Left, Fountains from the air, looking east. The river Skell on the right flows past the south side of the site, passing under bridges and through pipes before emerging at the far end. The various parts of the abbey can easily be identified by referring to the plan.

Opposite, the south aisle of Fountains, looking west. The vaulting—as at Fontenay—was by a series of transverse tunnel vaults of which only the lower parts now remain.

began to flow into the new abbey. 'Externally,' says Serlo with careful jubilation, 'the house was increased in wealth, much more internally in holiness.'

The buildings were begun about 1140 (there was a serious fire in 1145 but the damage was soon repaired); most of them were finished in about fifty years. To take the church first. The earliest part, the chancel, was altered (as we shall see), but the original form is known from excavations. It had one of the typical early Cistercian square plans and differed from that of Fontenay only in being rather shorter. Indeed it was simply the central and longest of seven straight-sided chapels opening off the east side of the transepts. The two outer pairs, the shortest, still remain. The arches into them are pointed, a very early use of this feature in England, though common enough in Burgundy, and they had pointed tunnel vaults, another Burgundian import. The north transept was originally the same as the south but has been greatly altered by Abbot Huby's tower (described later). Was there a central tower over the crossing? It seems so, although the Cistercian Rule forbade towers. Crossing towers were, however, usual in England, and this seems to be an example of the tenacity of local traditions in the face of an 'international' style from abroad.

The nave still has its arcades of pointed arches resting on sturdy round piers, and its clerestory. The aisles were vaulted with transverse pointed tunnel vaults, exactly as at Fontenay. A comparison of the ruins of Fountains with the complete version at Fontenay (described on p. 71) will immediately make clear how the former looked originally. At Fontenay, as we have seen, the function of these vaults (which were far more expensive than an ordinary wooden roof) was to buttress the high vault of the nave. But at Fountains there is no high vault and never was; the elevation makes no provision for it. This is one of the anomalies of Fountains and no satisfactory explanation has been found. Perhaps, again, it is the result of a compromise between the technical advice of Geoffrey of Clairvaux and native British conservatism.

There were five ways into the church on the south side, five doorways that tell us a great deal about the way life was lived there. In the south transept are the 'night' stairs, by which the monks could get quickly from their dormitory into the choir. Then in the south aisle, in the first bay west of the crossing, was the usual doorway into the cloister. Further west, at the other end of the aisle, are three more doors close together; the first was the 'night' stairs for the lay

brethren (whose dormitory, it will be remembered, always occupied the upper part of the west claustral range); the second led into the cellar underneath; and the third into a pentice running along the front of the west range, connecting the abbey with the guests' lodgings. All these will be described in more detail later. The west front, like that of Fontenay, lacks its original narthex, and has a huge Perpendicular window inserted in 1494. The original front would have looked more severe.

By 1200 the choir was found to be too small, a fairly common problem in Cistercian abbeys created by the preference (which we have already noted) for a large number of altars. Solutions varied. At Pontigny, founded shortly before Fountains, the enlarged east end was given the form of a chevet of chapels radiating from a semicircle. This was copied at several abbeys in England as well as in France. At Fountains a new eastern transept was added, an original idea copied very closely at Durham Cathedral a few years later but hardly anywhere else. The 'Chapel of the Nine Altars', as it is called, is perhaps the loveliest of all the buildings at Fountains. Begun shortly before 1210 and finished by 1247, it belongs to the first phase of Early English, with its pure, simple lines, lancet windows (without tracery) and slender vertical proportions. The

Below left, the cloister, looking into the south-east corner. Every trace of the covered walks themselves has disappeared. On the left are the arches leading to the chapter house; in the corner the stairs to the dormitory; next to it the door to the warming-room, with its chimney, and on the right the entrance to the refectory. Between these two doors are the remains of the monks' lavatorium.

Below, a view inside the warming-room. Here it was the custom for a fire to be lit on November 1st, All Saints' Day, and kept alight until Easter. There were originally two fireplaces: the one on the left has been blocked. The timber supports of the other are modern; the lintel originally stood unsupported.

Below right, the chapter house, looking east. It was vaulted and divided into three by two rows of columns.

Opposite, the dormitory, which originally occupied the whole upper floor of the east wing; the lower storey was a dark cellar. The chimney belongs to the warming-room.

contrast with the heavy transitional Romanesque of the main transepts and nave is still striking and must have been much more so when all were complete.

The rebuilding took in the whole church east of the crossing. The old chancel and the two flanking chapels were demolished and a new chancel of seven bays erected, ending in the second transept with the nine altars. Round the walls ran an arcade of trefoil-headed blank arches and the aisle windows above it were set inside graceful triple arches. The aisles, chancel and transept seem to have had quadripartite vaults. The high arcade of the clerestory continued across the eastern transept, supported on piers of extreme height and slenderness. They must originally have looked even finer, for they were surrounded by a cluster of eight smaller shafts of speckled Nidderdale marble; now only the bases and capitals of these subsidiary shafts are left. The now-vanished chancel arcade also had eight shafts per pier. The whole must have produced an extremely linear effect, reinforced by the lancet windows of the east, north and south (all altered and enlarged in the Perpendicular period). The east window had nine tall lancets; it must have looked rather like the transept of York with its 'Five Sisters'.

An interesting detail in the choir is the two pits on the north and

south side where the choir stalls used to stand. In them were placed earthenware pots to improve the acoustics—a somewhat unCistercian innovation made by the very unCistercian Abbot Huby about 1500.

Of the cloister nothing at all remains, which is surprising in such a well-preserved building. It seems to have been demolished deliberately in the 18th century to make a garden in the cloister-garth. The great cedar tree was planted at the same time. (Fountains was then the grandest of all 'Gothick ruins' to grace a gentleman's park; it belonged to the Studley Royal estate and its present ineffable picturesqueness is largely the result of the deliberate policy of the then owner, William Aislabie.)

The chapter house, on the east side, still has its triple entrance arches. Finished in about 1170, it was a large room of 18 bays, rib-vaulted and running, as usual, partly underneath the monks' dormitory, which occupied the upper storey of this whole range. At the end of the dormitory, and overhanging the river, were the monks' latrines, the *necessarium* or rere-dorter (behind-the-dormitory). The river, as again was usual in Cistercian abbeys, served a variety of purposes. As it flowed down from the west it supplied the monks with water for drinking, brewing and washing, turned their mill-wheel and finally flowed away to the east taking their sewage with it.

On the south side the main feature is the refectory, an early 13th-century building set, as at Fontenay and all Cistercian abbeys, at right angles to the cloister. Beside its doorway is the usual washing place (*lavatorium*). The first few bays of the refectory are windowless, since other buildings abut it on both sides, but further south it has tall shafted lancet windows. The reader's pulpit can just be recognised. Flanking the refectory were the warming-room (on the east) and the kitchen (on the west). The former is one of the best-preserved rooms at Fountains. It has a huge fireplace over 16 feet wide and is covered by a low rib vault. The monks could reach this room directly from the dormitory, a comfortable arrangement in winter when a fire (the only 'social' fire in the monastery) was kept burning day and night. The kitchen had a fireplace in the middle of the room, its ancient position. Monastic kitchens of this type survive elsewhere but the one at Fountains is today a mere shell.

The west range of the cloister, which projects as far again to the south in one long block, was the domain of the lay brothers. Their dormitory took up the upper storey; the ground floor, used partly as their refectory (served from the same kitchen as the monks')

Above, the refectory, which replaced an earlier hall in the 13th century. There was originally an arcade down the middle—the springing of an arch remains on the far wall.

Opposite, a view of the abbey, one of the most peaceful and romantic scenes in England. The romanticisation of Fountains goes back to the 19th century, when the ruins were deliberately integrated into a picturesque landscape, and it is still almost inescapable. But it should not be forgotten that Fountains was for the most of its history no place to enjoy the beauties of nature, a grim place in spite of its fine buildings, harassed by the elements, by the incursions of the Scots and by crushing debts. 81

Left, the undercroft of the west range, which belonged to the lay brothers. The floor above was their dormitory, now roofless. The ground floor, seen here, was divided between their refectory and the cellar.

The east end of Fountains was rebuilt between 1210–47 in an enlarged and wholly original way. The view, below, shows the north aisle of the new chancel (the main arcade has vanished) looking into the eastern transept, the Chapel of the Nine Altars.

Right, the Chapel of the Nine Altars, looking north. In the centre are the two very tall piers that carried the arcade across the transept— originally surrounded by slender shafts of marble.

and partly as a cellar, is almost intact—one of the most splendid examples of medieval functional building anywhere. The elements are completely simple—a row of central piers without capitals (common enough in England but on the continent a sure sign of post-14th-century work), plain chamfered ribs, lancet windows (or, in the northern section, still round-headed). The full extent of this range can best be appreciated by going outside the abbey buildings and looking back at the west front. With the church on one side and the wooded stream on the other, it forms a magnificent composition, representing, as Professor Pevsner says, 'a world of exacting order unmatched in the secular world'. Like the monks' dormitory, its further end projects over the stream and contains the latrines in a range to the west. Beyond that, still straddling the stream, was the lay brothers' infirmary and beyond this again the two blocks of apartments for guests. They could reach the church in comfort by using a long wooden covered way or pentice, which originally ran along the side of the whole west front; its doorway into the nave has been noticed earlier.

The monks' own infirmary lay at the opposite end of the abbey and was similarly built like a bridge across the stream. It had its own cellar, kitchen and chapel and was clearly a self-contained unit of some complexity but has now vanished almost entirely. Fountains Hall, the Jacobean mansion built after the Dissolution by the purchaser of the abbey, is mostly made out of stone from this part.

The impression gained from the ruins of Fountains today is of untroubled grandeur, security and peace. This picture is far from accurate. The abbey was harassed by troubles almost continuously from the middle of the 13th century to the time of the Dissolution. Its golden age had lasted not much more than a hundred years. Possibly the expenditure on building, which must have been very great, strained its resources. At any rate, by 1274 the abbey was borrowing money from the Jews of York. Fifteen years later it was in debt to the amazing sum of £6373, and an official was appointed by Edward I to remedy 'the impoverished condition into which it has fallen'. In the 14th century the incursions of the Scots and in the 15th the unrest that accompanied the Wars of the Roses both blighted its prosperity, although its possessions and 'granges' (estates lying at a distance from the abbey) were still very extensive indeed. By 1478 the church was beginning to fall down. Signs of repair work, more or less makeshift in character, are evident in many parts. A tower over the crossing, after first being raised to a dangerous height on piers inadequate for its support, was dismantled and a huge buttress built against one of the crossing piers. The stone vault of the choir was replaced by a wooden ceiling.

The 15th century saw the decline of the Cistercian Order, which was by now fatally compromised with worldly interests. Several splinter groups broke away, attempting to preserve or revive the old ideals, but Fountains was not one of them. In fact the story of the rule of the last three abbots is a strangely tragic one, of pride going before a fall. Marmeduke Huby was elected abbot in 1494 and it was he who was responsible for the most conspicuous part of the whole abbey and one which has so far hardly been mentioned —the great tower over the north transept. Such a tower was of course forbidden by earlier Cistercian decrees, but by this time these were little regarded. Huby even decorated it with his own coat-of-arms combined with quotations from the Cistercian breviary. It must be admitted that in itself it is a feature of great beauty, providing the monastic complex as a whole with just the aesthetic emphasis it needed. Huby carried out several other improvements and was undoubtedly a most able administrator, though he could hardly have sympathised very passionately with his predecessors' ideals.

The next abbot, William Thirsk, took part in the 'Pilgrimage of Grace', the rebellion in the north against Henry VIII's ecclesiastical policy, and was hanged. The last abbot surrendered his monastery to the king on November 26, 1539. There were 31 monks.

The east end of the abbey-church, seen from the river. In the foreground are the remains of the infirmary wing which was built out over the water; they give a good idea of the very efficient drainage that took in the whole of the south side of Fountains. Further back is the end wall of the Chapel of the Nine Altars (the huge central window is a later insertion), behind which stands the tall bell-tower, built (in defiance of the old Cistercian rules) by Abbot Huby.

CHAPTER 5

MAULBRONN:
THE CISTERCIANS IN GERMANY

An air view of Maulbronn from the west. In the background is part of the artificial lake made by the monks to help their water supply and drainage. In front of it is the church and monastery proper, and nearer the foreground the well-preserved estate buildings.

In 1110 monks from Cîteaux founded Morimond; in 1119 Morimond founded Bellevaux; in 1131 Bellevaux founded Neuburg in Alsace; Neuburg founded Maulbronn on the other side of the Rhine, in Württemberg. Such is Maulbronn's pedigree; but its foster-father, as it were, was a layman, the Swabian knight Walter von Lomersheim. In 1138 he decided to endow a Cistercian monastery on his own estates at Eckenweiher and to enter it himself. A party of monks under an abbot, Dieter, arrived in March. The first site chosen proved unsuitable and a few years later they moved to *Mulenbrunnen* ('Mill-well'), also in the district of Eckenweiher, though according to Bishop Günther of Speyer, who arranged the move, it was 'extremely wild and dangerous to all travellers because of attacks by robbers'. The new monastery was begun in 1147.

The site was carefully prepared for the accommodation of a large complex of buildings. Its water-supply, drainage and defence were expertly planned. To make a reservoir the monks dammed up a stream flowing down from the east (the water-level was as high as the roof of the buildings—a circumstance that does not seem to have worried them). From this artificial lake water flowed easily to wherever it was needed and also took care of the sewage. There was also a well for drinking water.

Maulbronn prospered from the beginning. This was the period of the Second Crusade, preached by St Bernard and therefore of special concern to the Cistercians. At Christmas 1146 he came to Bishop Günther's own cathedral of Speyer and persuaded King Conrad III to don the crusader's cross. All this benefited the new abbey. According to records, the bishop advanced money to prospective crusaders in return for a donation of land to the abbey. Other

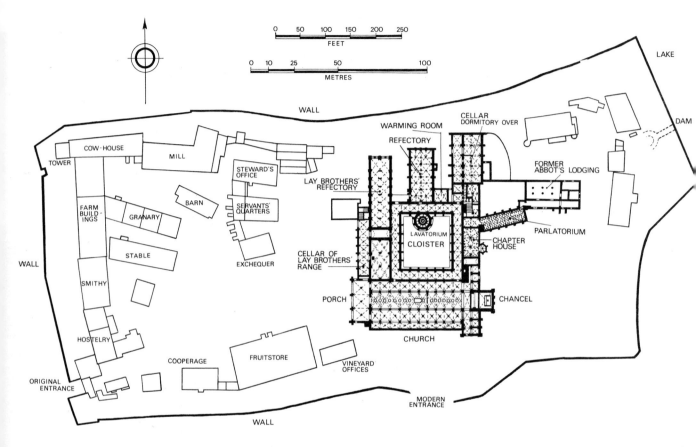

A plan of the monastic buildings at Maulbronn.

lavish gifts and bequests followed. Count Ludwig of Württemberg gave the abbey his estate at Elfingen; others gave farms, vineyards, even parts of towns (including Speyer). Eventually Maulbronn owned more than 100 properties on both sides of the Rhine. In 1148 it was taken under the protection of Pope Eugenius III, and ten years later under that of the Emperor Frederick Barbarossa. It was a favoured place, enjoying privileges of which older houses might well have been jealous. Daughter-abbeys were founded: Bronnbach in 1151, Schöntal in 1157.

The church and many of the claustral buildings date from this first period of Maulbronn's history. The plan of the church is based on that of Clairvaux, the classic Cistercian plan with a straight-ended chancel and a row of straight-ended chapels opening off the transepts by pointed arches. The transepts here are so narrow as to be little more than passages leading to the chapels and they open into the body of the church only through small doorways, so that from the nave there appear to be no transepts at all.

Building proceeded from east to west, ending with the west front, and the church was consecrated in 1178. It is an austere enough building. The effect of the nave arcade is rather that of a pierced wall than of a succession of architectural members. The piers are rectangular with attached demi-shafts on the east and west sides only. The arches are completely unmoulded. Above them comes an expanse of blank wall, which in a normal Romanesque church would have been plastered and frescoed, but not in a Cistercian. At the top is a row of plain narrow clerestory windows. The east window and the nave vault are much later additions. The original nave ceiling was of wood but there are heavy quadripartite rib vaults over the choir and the transept chapels. One of the remarkable features of Maulbronn is the survival of the 12th-century outer roof over the south transept. The west doors are also original; they are made of wood, covered with thick parchment, originally painted, over which the elaborate ironwork is fixed. Decoration, in accordance with the decrees of the General Chapters of this time, is kept to a minimum, but there are some attractive capitals with geometrical patterns in the eastern part. The stone pulpitum, which divides the church almost in the middle, is a rare Romanesque survival.

Four master-builders are associated with Maulbronn during the years 1147–1210, of whom the second and third (identifiable by such small indications as the profiles of the mouldings and the 'fish-bone' pattern of some of the stone-cutting) are thought to have come from Alsace. About 1210 a narthex (or 'galilee' or 'paradise') was added to the west front—a feature that has disappeared at both Fontenay and Fountains. Here it is a splendid loggia of three bays with simple quadripartite vaulting. It uses several features of French Gothic (already well established in the Ile de France), but all the arches are round. And in order that all these may rise to the same height the diagonal ribs spring from a point several feet lower than those parallel or at right angles to the walls.

The monastic buildings must have been planned in conjunction with the church. They are, unusually, on the north side, but otherwise the layout follows the standard Cistercian pattern as we have already seen it at Fontenay and Fountains, only 'north' becomes 'south' and vice versa.

The cloister as it now stands dates from various periods. The

The nave of the monks' church. To imagine it as it was in the 12th century one must discount the vault and traceried windows, which date from the 15th century. The vault of the choir, however, and—a rare survival—the choir screen or pulpitum are Romanesque.

Left, a view of the inside of the porch. The vault is curious: the architect retained round arches for both transverse and diagonal ribs, with the result that the latter, with their wider span, have to begin several feet lower down in order to rise to the same height as the former.

Below left, the south aisle, looking east. The contrast between the 12th and 15th century is again apparent. To the first belong the square piers on the left with their round arches; to the second the vault and the arches into the chapels on the right, through what was originally wall.

south walk is the earliest and most interesting. It was built about 1220—that is, 10 years after the narthex. Here the vault is sexpartite and a pointed arch is used for the transverse arches, so that they can spring from the same level as the diagonals. The north walk was transformed when the *lavatorium* was built. The west walk is late 13th century and the east dates from between 1400 and 1450.

This east walk of the cloister is the only one to have an upper storey. It formed part of the monks' dormitory, which occupied the whole upper part of this range. On the ground floor in the centre was the chapter house, which most unusually ran north–south instead of east–west (that is, it ran parallel with the cloister walk, not projecting at right angles to it). The present chapter house, with its elaborate star vault, dates from the early 15th century, but stands on the same site as the earlier one.

This wing, which included the dormitory, extended a good way beyond the cloister; its northern part consisted on the ground floor of a large cellar. The monks could enter the church by night stairs in the north transept. The monastic library was of a slightly later date, housed in a room above this transept.

The north range of the cloister is of great interest. Moving westwards the first room was the warming-room, a feature which we have already come across in other monasteries though that at Maulbronn must be unique. It is divided horizontally into two, the lower part consisting simply of a large stove. In its ceiling (that is, the floor of the room above) are drilled twenty holes a few inches in diameter, through which passed hot air—and, one imagines, a good deal of smoke as well—rather on the principle of a Roman hypocaust. The monks would have used the upper room for warming themselves in winter, for drying parchment, for mixing ink, and for the periodic blood-letting that was thought to be conducive to health in the middle ages. Another tube in the walls took some of the hot air to the refectory next door.

The refectory is architecturally the finest part of Maulbronn. Built towards the middle of the 13th century, it is a large hall, brilliantly lit on three sides by tall lancet windows. The vault, supported on an arcade running down the middle, is sexpartite, of which the transverse ribs are pointed, the diagonal round and the longitudinal ones stilted on little colonnettes above the main columns. The columns themselves are of two types, main and subsidiary, according to the ribs they carry. (The sequence of narthex,

Below left, the 15th-century east walk of the cloister, with (on the right) the entrance to the chapter house. The bay in the foreground belongs to the south walk of about 1220.

The chapter house, below, dates in its present form from the first half of the 15th century. Its vault is much less orthodox than it seems at first sight: basically, it consists of triangles instead of squares, so that piers stand opposite openings, not opposite other supports.

Opposite, the usual lavatorium, *opening off the cloister, here a charming 'fountain-chapel' (similar to that which once existed at Fontenay).*

Above left, the refectory, architecturally the finest part of Maulbronn and a perfect example of the transitional style between Romanesque and Gothic.

Left, the parlatorium, *a gallery connecting the abbot's lodging with the cloister, represents the end of the fascinating series of vaulting types at Maulbronn. It was built in 1493; the ribs rise straight from the shafts without capitals, and the whole vault has become merely an ornamental net unrelated to structure.*

Above, the refectory of the lay brothers. The low thick walls and crude windows belong to the earliest period at Maulbronn, the double-columns and groin vault (elliptical in section) to the mid-13th century.

91

south cloister and refectory shows the progressive adaptation of German Romanesque to the Gothic style, and may well represent the development of a single architect.) Originally there was a reader's pulpit. On the west side a hatch opened into the kitchen. The door into the refectory is in the centre—that is, immediately in line with the row of columns—an awkward arrangement forced upon the architect by the different bay widths of the refectory and cloister, which prevented him from placing the door to one side.

The west range, again as we should expect, was given over to the lay brothers. The ground floor consisted of two large rooms. The northernmost was the lay brothers' refectory and dates from about 1210; it is divided down the middle by a row of coupled columns supporting a groin vault (restored, like much else in this room). On the east side a hatch opened into the kitchen—another example (we saw it also at Fountains) of the same kitchen serving two refectories. The kitchen here has completely disappeared—one of Maulbronn's few casualties to time.

The west end of this range was a cellar, with the unusual feature of two doorways in the outside wall. It has heavy rib-vaulting and the floor is about four feet below ground level. Outside it a vaulted cloister walk (a rather luxurious version of the pentice that once existed at Fountains) was built in 1479, though its style is old fashioned for the period. It led to a 'winter refectory' constructed at one end of the lay brothers' dormitory—a piece of self-indulgence unthinkable among the early Cistercians. The dormitory took up the upper floor of this whole range. It was unvaulted (hardly any upstairs rooms in monasteries have a vault) and has been considerably altered in recent times.

The quantity of ornament in the monastic parts of Maulbronn increased with time, capitals and bosses becoming richer and more naturalistic. Some of the foliage carving is the equal of anything in England and France. About 1420 important additions were made to the church, reflecting the familiar story of the relaxation of Cistercian austerity. The nave was given a pretty 'net vault' and flying buttresses on the exterior to support it. Big Gothic windows with elaborate tracery were inserted in the choir, and a row of chapels was built along the south side, arches for them being cut in the wall of the south aisle.

The abbot's lodging, originally a Romanesque building of which some traces remain, was almost entirely rebuilt in 1512 by Abbot 92 Entenfuss. (His name means literally 'duck-foot': his rebus or

Between about 1450 and 1475 Maulbronn acquired new richly decorated choir stalls. The two scenes at the end of the south side, above, show the Drunkenness of Noah and David with the Ark of the Covenant.

The west front of Maulbronn. The Cistercians came to Germany during the lifetime of St Bernard. Maulbronn, begun in 1147, was one of the largest and most prosperous of their foundations and preserves several architectural features that have failed to survive elsewhere. Among them is the narthex, or west porch, where lay members of the abbey, guests and travellers could assemble before entering the church.

emblem, a duck's foot holding a crozier, appears on several parts of it.) It is a large, proud piece of work, which, in terms of its relation to the Cistercian ideal, may be compared to Huby's tower at Fountains. Connecting the abbot's house with the cloister is a pleasant vaulted gallery acting as the *parlatorium*. It looked out on to the abbot's garden and in its present form dates from 1493. Above it, of the same date and in the same style, is an oratory. Both have exquisite late Gothic vaults. The infirmary, which stood still further back to the east, was burnt down in 1892.

The area west of the monastery is taken up by the farm buildings. This is the side of monastic life of which we can read at length in the records, but which we tend to underemphasise because the material evidence has usually disappeared. In France and England there are some large medieval barns and a few mills—signs of a thriving agriculture equal or superior to any of the great secular estates—but nothing like Maulbronn, where the whole ensemble survives on a scale and in a condition that is unique.

The whole monastic area, including the church and cloister, is contained within a moat and wall dating from 1361–1441 though undoubtedly replacing very much older works. There are towers at irregular intervals; the only entrance was a gateway at the south-west angle, which had a drawbridge and a portcullis. (The present entrance to the abbey is in the south.)

A visitor coming in by the old gateway would find immediately on his left a small guest-house and the lodging (parts of which date back to the 13th century) for the priests whose duty it was to say early Mass in the small chapel opposite, the Chapel of the Trinity. The left-hand range (that is, the west side of the whole area) continued with the stables and coach-house, the smithy (early 16th century) and a barn, while at right angles to them were the granary, bakehouse and mews. Some of these have been changed (the mews is now the local town hall, and of the coach-house only a large round-arched entrance remains) but the general effect is still very impressive. The mews has a Renaissance gable front of 1588.

On the north side were cowsheds and the mill, the first of about 1440, and the second later, with Renaissance ornaments. Along the south wall stood the cooperage (where barrels were made), the fruit-store and wine-press, and the vineyard offices, all adapted in the 16th century from medieval buildings. The fruit-store especially is monumental, with a vast sloping roof extending down through six
94 storeys; there are two more floors below it, as well as a vaulted

The farm and estate buildings of Maulbronn have survived on a unique scale, as can be seen from the aerial view on p. 85. These three views show some of the most impressive examples. Far left, the fruit store and, left, the smithy, stables (with Renaissance gable) and granary, behind which rises the north-west tower of the old rampart. The view, below left, shows the buildings looking the other way, with the barn in the foreground, servants' building and exchequer behind, and in the background the church with its tall spire over the crossing.

cellar. The date—of the conversion from an earlier structure—is about 1580.

Three more large buildings form another range in the centre—the steward's office (mid-16th century), the servants' lodgings (bearing the date 1550 but this refers to its renovation only) and the administrative offices or exchequer (a 19th-century imitation in the old style). In the north-east corner is a ducal palace built about 1585–95 when control of the monastery had passed into lay hands.

Throughout most of the middle ages there was disagreement between the secular rulers who claimed rights over Maulbronn, though this does not seem to have affected the abbey's prosperity. The contenders were the Counts Palatine of the Rhine and the Count of Württemberg. In 1504 the Emperor Maximilian gave the patronage to Christof von Württemberg. During the religious wars of the 16th century the Cistercians were often in danger and were in fact expelled and restored again. By the Peace of Augsburg in 1555 Württemberg became Protestant, and Maulbronn, suppressed as a monastery, was refounded almost at once as a seminary. There was a brief Catholic restoration from 1629 to 1646, after which it reverted to being a seminary, which in fact it still is. Continuity of function added to Protestant allegiance have combined to save it from either of the two fates that overtook nearly every other monastery in Germany—ruin or Baroquification. It remains one of the best-preserved monastic complexes in the whole of Europe.

CHAPTER 6

POBLET:
THE CISTERCIANS IN SPAIN

The Cistercians came to Spain in 1131, when Alfonso VII of Castile and León invited St Bernard to send a party of monks from Clairvaux to Moreruela. They were immediately successful, as they always were, and soon rivalled the Benedictines, who had anyway made themselves unpopular in Spain. Poblet in Catalonia, near Barcelona, was founded in 1151. Its mother-house was Fontfroide in Languedoc and its patron was Ramón Berenguer IV, known as 'the saint', Count of Barcelona.

Poblet already enjoyed some celebrity as a hermitage and as the scene of several miracles associated with the Moorish invasion. In the mid-12th century the frontier with the Moors was still only some sixty miles away on the other side of the Ebro. Spain never lost the feeling that she was in the van of the crusade against the Infidel and that Christianity was essentially a battle. There is a ruthlessness and a passion in Spanish religion, and no less in Spanish monasticism, that distinguishes it from that of every other country in Europe. When one of the abbots of Poblet led the assault on Béziers during the Albigensian War of 1209, a group of citizens barricaded themselves in the church. 'Cut off all their heads,' he ordered, 'and then God can choose his own.'

Like Maulbronn, Poblet was favoured from the beginning by lavish support from the local nobility. Many of the monks were men of high birth. Abbot Amalrich, just mentioned, was descended from the Dukes of Narbonne. A son of Alfonso II of Aragon took his vows there in 1201. Abbot Hostalrich was a close friend of King Jaime I, *El Conquistador*, and it was at Poblet that they planned the conquest of Majorca in 1228. Jaime wished to end his life as a novice at Poblet but left it too late and died on the way. He was not the

The entrance to the abbey-church of Poblet, in Catalonia, illustrates the contrast—familiar all over Europe—between the austerity of early Cistercian ideals and their subsequent worldliness. When first built the west front of the nave (seen here with half of its rose window peering over the wall) was a place of embattled faith behind a double rampart of defences. In the 18th century, when the new Baroque front was added, it had become a centre of cultured, conservative prestige.

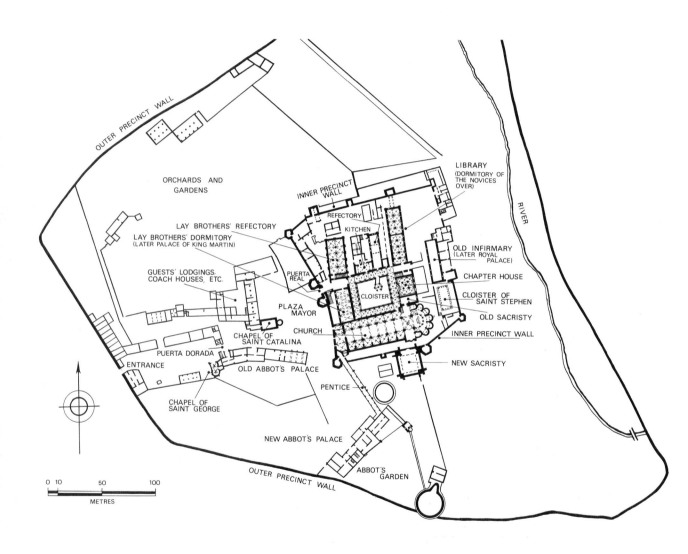

OUTER PRECINCT WALL

ORCHARDS AND
GARDENS

LAY BROTHERS' REFECTORY

LAY BROTHERS' DORMITORY
(LATER PALACE OF KING MARTIN)

GUESTS' LODGINGS,
COACH HOUSES, ETC.

PLAZA
MAYOR

PUERTA
REAL

INNER PRECINCT
WALL

REFECTORY

KITCHEN

LIBRARY
(DORMITORY OF
THE NOVICES
OVER)

RIVER

OLD INFIRMARY
(LATER ROYAL
PALACE)

CHAPTER HOUSE

CLOISTER

CLOISTER OF
SAINT STEPHEN

OLD SACRISTY

INNER PRECINCT WALL

CHURCH

CHAPEL OF
SAINT CATALINA

PUERTA DORADA

ENTRANCE

OLD ABBOT'S PALACE

CHAPEL OF
SAINT GEORGE

PENTICE

NEW SACRISTY

NEW ABBOT'S PALACE

ABBOT'S
GARDEN

OUTER PRECINCT WALL

0 10   50   100
|—|——|————|————————|
METRES

A plan of the monastery of Poblet.

first king to be buried there. Alfonso II had preceded him in 1196 and it later became one of the accepted burial places of the Aragonese royal house. Poblet was a *real monasterio*, a royal monastery; it paid no taxes and had the right to display the royal coat of arms. And since it was on one of the main Roman roads of Spain, the Via Aurelia between Taragona and Lérida, its fame and wealth were increased by travellers and by important people who used it as a staging post.

The church and monastic buildings constructed during this early period are on a scale befitting Poblet's position. The style is basically identical with the Cistercian buildings of France, though (as in England and Germany) local tradition exercised some influence. The cloister, as at Maulbronn, lies on the north, and the claustral buildings are surrounded by a high wall. Outside this wall extensive outbuildings existed—stables, guest-houses, hospital, servants' quarters as well as gardens and orchards—and these are again surrounded by another wall nearly a mile in circumference. In the following description we shall deal with the monastery proper first and the rest later, which is also roughly the order in which they were built.

The church dates from 1180–96—that is, some thirty years after the foundation of the abbey. The east end has a chevet of chapels (as at Pontigny) rather than the bleak straight end of Fontenay and (originally) Fountains. Its architectural impact, however, is entirely lost today because of the hugh Renaissance retable that now stands behind the altar and reaches nearly to the vault. The nave recalls Fontenay very strongly—the same bareness, the same slightly pointed arcade with double unmoulded arches, almost the same pier-section, the same shafts rising from floor to ceiling, the same pointed tunnel vault with transverse arches. The only important differences are that Poblet has a clerestory whereas Fontenay has none, and that the aisles are covered by quadripartite rib vaults instead of transverse tunnels. Although Poblet is fifty years later than Fontenay, all this would have looked distinctly old fashioned in France. The west front originally had one of the standard Cistercian porches, which here was part of the encircling wall of the inner precinct, a curious and one would have thought self-defeating arrangement. In the early 18th century a new (or rather, false) Baroque front was substituted. It had statues, coloured marbles and bronze doors but is now sadly decayed.

Of the Romanesque cloister in its original form only one side

Poblet from the south, surrounded by what used to be its estates. Towards the centre can be seen part of the old abbey wall, with a tower at each end. To its right is the church, the crossing tower partly hidden by the square bulk of the New Sacristy. 99

survives: that on the south, against the church. Like the church itself, it has plain pointed arches but the impression of austerity is mitigated by the twin colonnettes that subdivide each opening. The other three sides were reconstructed during the 13th century; the openings were filled with tracery and new vaults were inserted. The walls were lined with the tombs and monuments of noble families and the whole cloister originally had a second storey of which only fragments now remain.

Of the buildings surrounding the cloister almost all date from the late 12th century or early 13th century and form one of the most complete ensembles of this date in Spain, or indeed in Europe. The ground floor of the east wing contains the chapter house (a square room of nine bays, the rib vaults supported on elegant octagonal piers) and the library, similar in style though cruder in its details. The upper floor of this wing is taken up by what has been called 'probably the most imposing dormitory ever erected by the Cistercian Order', the Dormitory of the Novices. It is a single vast room spanned by 19 pointed diaphragm arches upon which the rafters of the roof rest directly; the arches come down to plain corbels half-way up the wall. In the lower part there are two windows per bay—one between every pair of beds—and in the upper, one window per two bays. In its stark, functional simplicity this room is highly reminiscent, in spite of its different idiom, of one of the superb warehouses of the early Industrial Revolution. Against the east wall, at the end nearest the church, are built the archives and treasury.

The main building on the north side is the refectory, another bare stone room that seems to express the very spirit of St Bernard. It has a pointed tunnel vault, like the church, and at the north end steps in the wall lead to the reader's pulpit. Outside the doorway in the cloister, the monks' washing place or *lavatorium*, has a six-sided fountain house very like the original version of the one we have already seen at Maulbronn. Its style is that of the old Romanesque cloister of which it formed part.

Next to the refectory is the kitchen, a room of outstanding interest since so many monastic kitchens have fallen into ruin. It is oblong in shape covered by a rib vault with an open louvre in the centre for ventilation. On one side it communicates with the refectory, on the others with a store room and a courtyard where sheep and pigs were slaughtered (the stone butchers' tables still remain). The great fireplace is structurally separate, opening into the kitchen through a broad pointed arch.

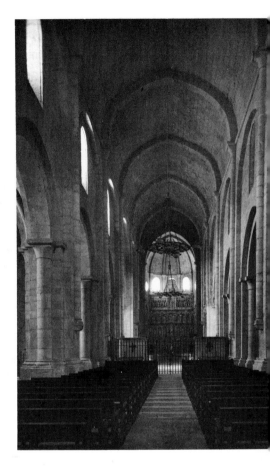

Above, the interior of the nave. Like Fontenay in its general features and absence of decoration, the presence of a clerestory gives it a rather lighter effect. Both clerestory and arcade are enclosed in one large unmoulded arch.

Above right, the west porch of the church, which formed part of the monastery's inner rampart. In 1720 the old front was replaced by a sumptuous Baroque entrance. The difference between old and new masonry is easy to see. In the niche above the gate is the Assumption of the Virgin, and beside it stand St Benedict and St Bernard.

In the west wing were the lay brothers' refectory (later used as a cellar) and dormitory (later the wine-press), and upstairs another dormitory for the fully professed monks, constructed on principles similar to that of the larger dormitory but with the diaphragm arches resting on piers down the middle, the whole row forming a sort of archless 'arcade'.

The whole precinct, as we have seen, was surrounded by a wall, which in its present form dates from the early 14th century. It was entered by the so-called Royal Gate, the *Puerta Real*, built by Pedro IV, nicknamed 'the Ceremonious'. The abbey at this period was still expanding on royal patronage, although its wealth did not always conduce to peace. About 1311 (when there were 88 monks

Above, the vast retable added in 1529, which completely contradicts the Cistercian austerity of the rest of the church. It was the work of Damián Forment of Valencia. The bottom section consists of garlands of fruit and flowers between pilasters. Then come five reliefs in conch-headed niches representing scenes from the Passion. Above these stand the Virgin and Child flanked on each side by three saints. Next, in seven niches, come the Seven Joys of Mary, the Resurrection being in the centre, separated by pilasters with figures of saints in front. On the next level is Christ Blessing and the twelve Apostles surmounted by the Crucifixion.

Opposite, the east walk of the cloister. The clustered colonnettes with their capitals of tight interlace belong to the original 12th-century work; the vault and tracery are 13th century.

Left, the chapter house looking east. Under the window can be seen the gravestones of some of the many abbots of Poblet who were buried here. On the far side part of the stone bench that went all round the room remains.

Below, the library, formerly one of the splendours of Poblet, now mostly restored from ruin. In 1753 it was catalogued as containing nearly four thousand volumes.

and 85 lay brothers) Poblet received a munificent gift of land in the city of Barcelona itself. Five years later the 'complement' of the abbey is listed as 95 monks, 55 lay brothers, 63 *cautivos* (presumably Moorish prisoners) and 100 animals. The next abbot was the great Copons, a close friend of the king (who gave him a large part of the royal library) and for some time his almoner. Copons died in the Black Death of 1348, along with 59 other monks and 30 lay brothers.

The royal apartments at Poblet form two main groups. The earliest were built next to the old infirmary buildings east of the church where there was a small cloister and a chapel dedicated to St Stephen. (This pre-dates the main cloister and the church and was the original nucleus of the whole monastery.) As time went by the 'palace' gradually replaced the infirmary. By the end of the 14th century, however, something grander was needed and a new palace

Above, the refectory, almost exactly as it was in the 12th century. Cistercian building followed a standard formula throughout Europe, and the early refectories of France, England and Germany were no doubt almost identical with this. On the right, projecting from the thickness of the wall, is the reader's pulpit.

Left, the dormitory of the novices—the noblest of all surviving monastic dormitories. Its wide roof carried on diaphragm arches is characteristic of Spanish Gothic. Decoration is confined to the basket-work patterns of the corbels.

Right, the monks' washing-place (lavatorium) projected into the cloister-garth opposite the entrance to the refectory. When most of the cloister was altered in the 13th century, this 'fountain-house' was left in its Romanesque form. Behind it rises the stark wall of the novices' dormitory.

was built in a rather awkward position in the west range of the cloister. This belongs to the reign of King Martin (1396–1414). It has a tiny courtyard and a pretty exterior staircase leading up to the first floor. The windows are filled with delicate lace-like tracery.

At a slightly earlier date (1367) the royal tombs in the transepts of the church had been given a more elaborate treatment. The spectacular 'royal pantheons' consisted of tombs built out on bridges between the piers of the crossing. Each tomb-chest was decorated with miniature arcades and mourners; the effigy (tilted, so as to be visible from below) lay under a high traceried canopy. They must have provided a curious contrast to the bareness of the church. The space underneath the 'bridges' was later filled in by sumptuous Renaissance sculpture, of which much remains.

Poblet was now among the most magnificent abbeys of Europe, and seemed destined to continue so indefinitely. But its fortunes were bound up with the royal house of Aragon. In 1469 King Ferdinand married Isabella of Castile and thenceforward Spain was, in theory at least, a united country. No more kings were buried at Poblet. Royal patronage in the succeeding years was lavished on the new capital of Madrid and on the Escorial. Poblet, however, retained its prestige. In 1493 the 'Catholic monarchs', Ferdinand and Isabella, paid it a ceremonial visit with their court. The 94 monks and 135 lay brothers entertained a company about five times their own number, including 500 ladies, who were lodged in a vast dormitory in the abbot's palace, their beds separated, we are told, by silk hangings. In 1546 Philip II passed Holy Week here, piously washing the feet of 13 poor men and serving them with food.

Outside the main precinct lay whole ranges of outbuildings for the running of the estate and the reception of guests. The present remains are mostly late in date, but buildings of similar function probably occupied the same sites throughout Poblet's history.

Entering the main gate of the whole monastery the visitor was faced by a straight avenue of trees. To the left were stables, smithies and servants' quarters, now all in ruins. Ahead was the *Puerta Dorada* (Golden Gate), a late 15th-century gateway, which at the time of Philip's visit was decorated with gilded bronze plaques. In the small atrium in front of the gate is the Chapel of St George (or of the Rosary), built by Alfonso V about 1442 to celebrate his accession to the throne of Naples.

Inside the *Puerta Dorada* were, on the right, women's quarters (for the retinue of important visitors), coach-houses, workmen's

Above, the kitchen, one of Poblet's most interesting survivals. In this view we are looking towards the main fireplace at the west end, with the chimney-flue exposed above it.

Opposite, the older monks' dormitory, a variant version of the structural system used in the dormitory of the novices. This room was formerly divided into cubicles, and grooves in the floor still mark the position of party-walls. 107

lodgings and guest-houses (up to the 16th century this was the site of the abbot's house). On the left was a group of buildings that included the bursar's office, a hospice for the poor, warehouses and the small chapel dedicated to St Catalina—one of the oldest buildings at Poblet, dating from the foundation of the abbey in 1151. Between this and the monastery wall is the large courtyard known as the *Plaza Mayor*.

In the extreme south of the whole area one of the abbots, Oliver (1583–98), built himself a grandiose new palace in the early Renaissance style. It had large rooms lined with polished stone, a monumental staircase and an upper loggia looking out over the countryside. (It is interesting to compare the apartments of Abbot Entenfuss at Maulbronn, of almost exactly the same date.) The palace, which was never finished, was linked to the church in the 18th century by a long covered passage or pentice through the garden.

The greatest monument of the 18th century is the New Sacristy, added to the south transept between 1732 and 1736. It is a large square room covered by a cupola and surmounted on the exterior by a heavy but elegant lantern. Inside, the architecture is chastely neo-classical but the original furnishings had a touch of Baroque abandon. There were gilded wooden doors; huge walnut chests under cupboards with Venetian glass doors; bright paintings of Cistercian saints; a polygonal chest in the centre for copes; and velvet hangings trimmed with gold and silver.

The New Sacristy marks the end of Poblet's glory. With the French Revolution and the succeeding wars Poblet was occupied by troops and her treasures scattered. In 1821, a time of continuing disorder in Spain, the abbey was pillaged by the local people. By 1835 it had become impossible to carry on monastic life and at the end of July, after a sad farewell service, the last monks evacuated it. As soon as it was empty, every movable object was stolen, the furnishings chopped down, the stone carted away, the grills and bells broken up and sold for scrap. Even the royal tombs were opened and gruesome scenes were enacted with the bones and mummified bodies.

Poblet remained in this state for almost exactly a century. It was left to the piety of General Franco and his régime to carry out some basic repairs to the buildings and to re-establish a small monastic community there. The monastery's immediate future, at least, seems fairly secure.

Looking into the cloister of St Stephen, a corner of Poblet that was repeatedly rebuilt in the middle ages and badly damaged in the 19th century. It was originally among the oldest parts of the abbey and the Romanesque arcade can still be seen, restored. Behind it is the crossing tower of the church, its windows once enriched with Late Gothic tracery, and behind that the lantern-top of the New Sacristy.

CHAPTER 7

ASSISI:
THE ORDER OF ST FRANCIS

There is no need to retell the familiar story of St Francis. In the present context we need only note that he takes his place as one of a line of reformers and religious leaders—Benedict, Odo of Cluny, Bernard of Clairvaux—who tried to free themselves from the corrupting burden of material possessions by a communal life based on work, worship and poverty. All had finally been defeated by the responsibility that possessions, even those held in common, brought with them. Now came Francis. When he said poverty he meant poverty.

In its pristine form the Franciscan ideal was one of absolute destitution: the friars were to live in hovels of wood and straw, wear clothes that would be thrown away by everyone else, eat anything that people gave them, own no property, accept no money. But this way of life entailed a complete absence of organisation, and as the numbers of Francis's followers grew and as they were forced to work out some kind of relationship with the Church and with society, the first sweeping simplification had to go. There is an enormous difference between the Rule that Francis formulated in 1209 when he had only a handful of disciples and that of 1223, drawn up with papal assistance, which was to be the charter of the Franciscan Order from then on. There is no doubt that this occurred with Francis's co-operation, if also with his regret. But when he died in 1226 his followers were faced with the choice of continuing in the same direction or of trying to go back to their founder's first inspiration. In fact they did both. They split. The unhappy story of the Franciscan movement in the 13th and 14th centuries is an extraordinary mixture of charity and rancour, of unworldly ideals and acrimonious bitterness.

The monastery of San Francesco at Assisi, 'head and mother' of the Franciscan order, is built on the steep side of an Umbrian hill-town, which is still almost unchanged since the middle ages. It is two churches in one. The lower piazza (in the foreground) leads the pilgrim to the porch of the lower church, while on the right, reached by a flight of steps, is the façade of the upper. The architecture, though influenced by French Gothic, has none of the lightness and aspiration that we associate with that style. On the left, buttressed by a triple-arcaded sub-structure, the monastic buildings look out across the valley.

111

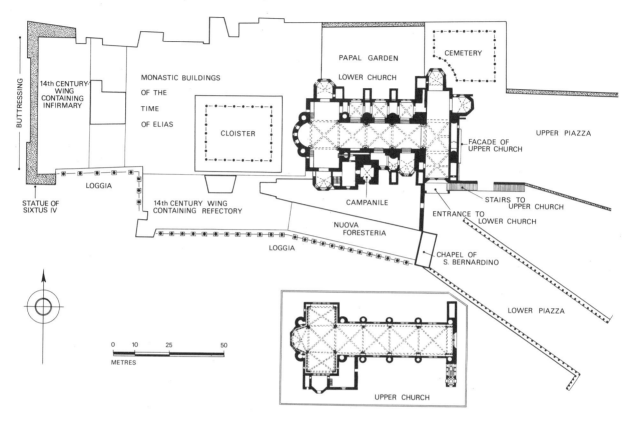

BUTTRESSING

14th CENTURY WING CONTAINING INFIRMARY

MONASTIC BUILDINGS
OF THE
TIME
OF ELIAS

CLOISTER

PAPAL GARDEN

LOWER CHURCH

CEMETERY

UPPER PIAZZA

FACADE OF
UPPER CHURCH

LOGGIA

STATUE OF
SIXTUS IV

14th CENTURY WING
CONTAINING REFECTORY

CAMPANILE

STAIRS TO
UPPER CHURCH

ENTRANCE TO
LOWER CHURCH

NUOVA
FORESTERIA

LOGGIA

CHAPEL OF
S. BERNARDINO

LOWER PIAZZA

0   10   25   50

METRES

UPPER CHURCH

Above, a plan of the monastery of San Francesco at Assisi at the level of the lower church. The upper church, built exactly above the lower, is shown in the inset.

Left, Assisi from the south. The town, of which a few buildings can be seen on the right, was in the 13th century much smaller and completely separate from the monastery. The tower is contemporary with the church and was finished in 1239.

112

One party believed in complete fidelity to the rule of poverty, the other advocated only so much poverty as was consistent with the growth of the order, its expansion to other countries, its missionary work and entry into the schools and universities. The second view was championed, with what to many appeared unseemly zeal, by Brother Elias, the real administrator of the order since Francis's return from the East in 1220. But at the first General Chapter, held the year after Francis's death in 1227, Elias was not confirmed in his office. Instead a more moderate man, Giovanni Parenti, was elected minister general.

The idea of honouring St Francis by building a magnificent church dedicated to his name was a perfectly natural one. He had been popularly regarded as a saint even in his lifetime, and the campaign to build the basilica was instigated at least as much by the people of Assisi and the pope (Gregory IX, formerly Cardinal Ugolino, Francis's friend and associate in drawing up the Rule) as by the Franciscans themselves, many of whom always doubted its fitness. Elias, the moving spirit though out of office, seems to have taken it largely upon himself. Fund raising was managed in Rome. Two citizens of Assisi donated the site.

Gregory himself came to Assisi with a train of cardinals in 1228 and on July 17, the day after St Francis's canonisation, he laid the foundation stone, declaring the Church to be the 'head and mother of the whole order. The work was pushed forward with tremendous speed and the unusual idea of the upper and lower churches must have been drawn up at the outset. In less than two years the lower church was sufficiently well advanced to receive the saint's body.

San Francesco stands at the extreme west end of the hill of Assisi. The lower church has no main front. It seems to burrow into the hill. The visitor comes into the south end of the eastern transept, turns to the left and sees the cruciform church before him—nave, crossing and apse. The proportions are wide and low, with rib vaults springing from close to the ground. The total impression is dark and crypt-like. In style, apart from the ribs of the vault there is no trace of the Gothic economy and elegance that was being exploited to such effect at this time in France and England. All the arches are round (some segmental) and there are heavy tunnel vaults over the transepts. The decoration on the walls and ceiling belongs to later times, and in 1230 it must have provided a stark setting for the translation of the body of St Francis to its new burial place under the crossing.

The only portrait of St Francis that has any claim to have been painted during his lifetime is this fresco in a chapel at Subiaco. It is said to have been done by a Benedictine monk when St Francis visited the abbey of Subiaco in 1218. There was, however, no tradition of realistic portraiture at this time, and one cannot assume that it is a reliable likeness.

113

Above, the lower piazza, where pilgrims gathered and still gather. In the centre can just be seen the entrance to the lower church. From here a flight of steps leads up to the façade of the upper church with its rose window and gable.

Left, the crossing of the lower church, looking north, with frescoes by the school of Giotto in the vault. It was here, in 1230, that the body of St Francis was brought and buried in circumstances of such mystery.

Above left, a view from the door of the lower Church, looking north. The chapel at the far end is later than the central bay, which was originally much darker; the frescoes are also 14th and 15th century. The main body of the lower church is to the right.

The ceremony did not pass off without disorder. What really happened is obscure, but it seems that Elias persuaded some of the townspeople to bring the body to the basilica three days before the date fixed by the friars, and to bury it in secret. The friars, though cheated of the vital particular, nevertheless held the ceremony as intended, but at the subsequent chapter meeting a violent quarrel broke out. Elias's party attempted to install him as minister general in place of Giovanni Parenti but were defeated. Elias was sent to a hermitage to do penance and a deputation of eminent friars was despatched to Rome to lay their complaints before the pope.

Clearly matters had reached an *impasse*. The issue was fundamentally one of principle, not of personalities. Gregory IX, in an attempt to reconcile the two factions, redefined the constitution of the order. Money donated to it, he decided, was to be administered by an agent or *nuntius*, to whom the friars could apply for 'imminent necessities'. What constituted imminent necessity was left to the senior members of the order. In effect this meant that it had money at its disposal in exactly the same way as any other order, only with a more cumbersome machinery for spending it. The question of houses and movable goods was left slightly more ambiguous. Friars were to have the *use* of these things, though strictly speaking they could not *own* them. Thus, their property had to be held legally in the name of the Holy See, or of a private benefactor or sometimes of a trustee appointed by the friars. St Francis's marriage with the Lady Poverty, in fact, was leading to nothing more than a tangle of legal fictions.

Such controversies did not prevent the Franciscans from expanding with phenomenal speed. Convents were established in England, France, Spain and Germany within a decade of St Francis's death. The order became especially notable for its learning, and Franciscan teachers were soon part of the intellectual life of Europe. In 1232 Parenti was forcibly retired and Brother Elias, more in sympathy with the way things were moving, took his place. Probably the majority of the friars supported him, but it was embarrassing that nearly all the Franciscan 'old guard', the close friends and associates of St Francis, took the opposite point of view. The split was not closed. The wound was not healed. But work on the great basilica of Assisi went on.

The form that it was taking was without parallel in Italy. Exactly over the lower church was built a far taller and lighter upper church. This had five bays (counting the crossing), transept and apse, like

The upper church, in contrast to the lower, was from the first light and cheerful. The nearest parallels to its architectural style are French; in Anjou, however, the sides would have been filled with blank arcading. Here they are left flat for the favourite Italian form of decoration—fresco.

115

the substructure below. It had no aisles, so apart from the transept it was one single unified space, unbroken except by the divisions of the vault. The most obvious models are the Romanesque churches of Anjou, especially the 12th-century cathedral of Angers. The upper church proceeded at the same rapid pace as the lower and was practically finished by 1239, though consecration was delayed until 1253. The Gothic style, whose structural advantages were being adopted by Italian architects without any real sympathy for their aesthetic qualities, plays hardly any part in the final effect. Admittedly, arches are pointed, the vault has ribs and the thrust is borne by external buttresses. But the wide proportions are still Romanesque in feeling, the ribs thick and very simply moulded, and the buttresses consist of solid semi-cylindrical masses of brick, though a couple of crude flying buttresses were later added on the south side.

The convent, which was built at the same time, lies behind the church, on the steep western slope of the hill. Its 'ground' floor is level with the lower church. To make a reasonably spacious area behind the church the foundations had to be built up with huge substructures. It was formerly much more isolated from the town of Assisi than it is now, and must have looked more like a castle than the shrine of a saint—so much so that Innocent IV actually used it to house the papal treasure when he was forced to flee from Rome.

The cloister lying immediately behind the apse is the oldest part, some fragments of it remaining from the time of Elias. (The stormy chapter meeting of 1230 was held at the convent, so building must have been fairly well advanced.) The second court, which required even more massive buttressing, was built later. Its furthest and highest corner (on the south-west) contained the infirmary and was built between 1343 and 1377 with money given to the order by Cardinal Albornoz. When that was finished a whole new range was added to the south side, entailing yet another substructure. It housed the Great Refectory, and the ranges of arches supporting it form an arcaded walk or loggia with superb views over the valley. During the 15th century this refectory range was joined to the piazza in front of the lower church by another wing, also supported on arches, known as the *Nuova Forestiera*. At its eastern end stands the little chapel of San Bernardino, built next to the door of the lower church in 1488 to commemorate St Bernardino's visit to Assisi in 1425.

In the 1470s the infirmary range showed signs of collapse. It was restored and strengthened by Sixtus IV, himself a Franciscan, whose

architect (said by Vasari to have been Baccio Pintelli, though his name does not appear in the documents) shored up the weak spot with a huge sloping buttress and built similar stone ramps on the north and west sides. In the buttress beneath the infirmary he placed a monumental niche, whence a statue of the pope gazes across the countryside. Pintelli also entirely rebuilt the two-storey arcade of the main cloister, added the entrance doorway and porch to the lower church (1478) and built a flight of steps from the lower piazza to the façade of the upper.

The most modern part of the whole monastery is the tomb of St Francis. As we have seen, the burial of 1230 had been secret and hurried. In 1442 the friars maintained that they did not know the exact location. A partial search in 1607 yielded no result. In 1814, however, a more thorough excavation was carried out and the body was found in a coffin enclosed by an iron cage. It was thought desirable to expose the saint to more public veneration and a new crypt was built for this purpose beneath the lower church. Designed in a rather pompous neo-classical style, it was finished in 1824. Though out of keeping with its surroundings and of little architectural merit, the descent from one crypt to another yet deeper can still arouse a feeling of irrational awe.

Opposite, the monastery from the west. (San Francesco is not orientated in the usual way and the 'west' front faces east.) The big sloping buttresses belong to the 1470s. To the left, higher up the hill, is the tower of the old Rocca or fortress of Assisi.

Left, one of the arcades that run all along the south side of the monastic buildings. These are really buttresses to support the sub-structure, but they form a delightful walk or 'loggia' with a view across the whole valley.

Below, the cemetery, a peaceful spot to the north of the church, which has hardly changed in seven hundred years. The first grave there is dated 1245.

San Francesco is of course most famous for its frescoes. A tantalising scarcity of documents makes them a subject of extraordinary complication, but during the years 1280–1320 the church at Assisi, again under the active stimulus of the popes, was the focus of some of the most talented artists of Rome, Umbria and Tuscany—perhaps Cavallini, perhaps Giotto, almost certainly Cimabue and certainly Simone Martini and the Lorenzetti brothers.

Cimabue of Florence probably came about 1280. To him are attributed the *Virgin and Child with St Francis* in the lower church (the figure of St Francis has been repainted several times) and a whole cycle of frescoes in the upper church transepts and crossing; they include Apocalyptic scenes, scenes from the Passion and the lives of the Virgin, St Peter and St Paul, but are all now in a bad state of preservation. Next came the upper parts of the nave walls. Those on one side tell the story of the Creation, Adam and Eve,

Cain and Abel, Noah, Abraham, Isaac and Jacob. Those on the other are devoted to the life of Christ. The style is that of the contemporary Roman school.

Last in the decorative scheme of the upper church are the St Francis cycle—a series of 28 large frescoes telling the story of St Francis's life from his youth in Assisi to his foundation of the order, his receiving the stigmata, his death and posthumous miracles. Many of these scenes have a clarity of composition, a realism and a sense of drama that had hardly been seen in painting before. The date seems to be somewhere in the 1290s. They made an immediate impact; they fixed the iconography of the Franciscan legend for ever and were imitated in Franciscan churches up and down Italy. They have long been attributed to Giotto. But did Giotto paint them? They are certainly unique, in monastic history as in the history of painting, and perhaps nowhere does the union of art and religion express a more urgent and explicit message than at Assisi. Nothing detracts from the simple message of the frescoes, which is also the message of the Franciscan Order. Here aesthetic and didactic appeal are one.

More work followed in the lower church. Painters of the school of Giotto decorated the vault above the crossing with allegories of the Franciscan virtues. Later, when the side chapels were built, Simone Martini and Pietro and Ambrogio Lorenzetti of Siena were among the painters chosen to decorate them. Almost equally outstanding is the 13th-century stained glass and the later carved stalls of the choir. San Francesco is indeed rich; it needs no special taste for paradox to wonder how its patron saint would have judged it.

To return, finally, to the story of the Franciscan movement itself. Strife between the Spirituals, or strict followers of St Francis, and the Conventuals, who favoured a more orthodox monastic constitution, continued throughout the 13th and 14th centuries. Successive popes were continually being asked for a clearer definition of the Rule and inclined to one side or the other according to temperament. By the beginning of the 16th century there was in effect not one Franciscan Order but two (more, if one counted all shades of opinion). In 1517 Leo X accepted the inevitable and divided them into two separate and distinct orders: the Observants, pledged to a strict observance of the Rule, and the Conventuals, who enjoyed the same rights and privileges as other orders. The monastery of Assisi became the headquarters of the Conventuals and so, with a few interruptions and suppressions by the state, it has remained.

The frescoes of San Francesco make it one of the key sites in the history of Western art. This view of part of the north wall gives an idea of the paintings in their setting. At the level of the windows are some of the badly preserved Old Testament series (top left, the Sacrifice of Isaac). Below these is the St Francis cycle, thought to be by Giotto, with three large scenes in each bay. The first three show St Francis at prayer, when he heard a voice from the crucifix bidding him repair a ruined church; then the saint, clad only in a blanket, renouncing his family and possessions; and third the dream of Pope Innocent III, who saw in sleep 'a little poor man' holding up his tottering church of the Lateran.

CHAPTER 8

THE CERTOSA, PAVIA:
RENAISSANCE CARTHUSIANS

The Carthusian Order was another quest for simplicity, for life reduced to the essentials. To trace its foundations we have to go back to the late 11th century.

In 1077 Bruno Hartenfaust, the son of one of the leading families of Cologne, a famous scholar, Chancellor of Reims and, had he wished, the next bishop, decided to abandon the world and devote himself to religion. It was not until 1088 that he was able to extricate himself from his responsibilities. He then went, with six companions, to the wild country of the French Alps, and at Chartreuse, on a site given to him by the Bishop of Grenoble, he established the first house of what was to grow into the Carthusian Order.

Chartreuse was as inhospitable a place as one could possibly choose. Steep, rocky and cold, it was very frequently under snow and virtually cut off from the rest of the world for weeks at a time. Nor in the eyes of the people of the 11th century did it have any of the romantic charm with which we invest it today. A French traveller of the pre-Wordsworthian age wrote: 'I cannot conceive how it could enter into the mind of man to establish a community in a spot so horrible and barren as this.' Bruno inevitably began with the Rule of St Benedict, but instead of adding to it, as most monks were tempted to do, he subtracted. There is a vivid description of life at the Chartreuse a few years after Bruno's death by Guibert, Abbot of Nugent:

'The church stands upon a ridge. . . . Thirteen monks live there and they have a fairly convenient cloister, but they do not live together like other monks. Each has his own cell round the cloister and in these they work, sleep and eat. On Sunday

The nave, looking north-east. Although the result of various compromises and changes of plan, the church of the Certosa gives an effect of powerful unity. The sexpartite vault can just be seen between the piers.

The dome over the crossing. Here one can clearly see Renaissance motifs taking over from Gothic. An elegant little gallery supports the octagonal vault, decorated at the end of the 16th century with scenes from the Apocalypse.

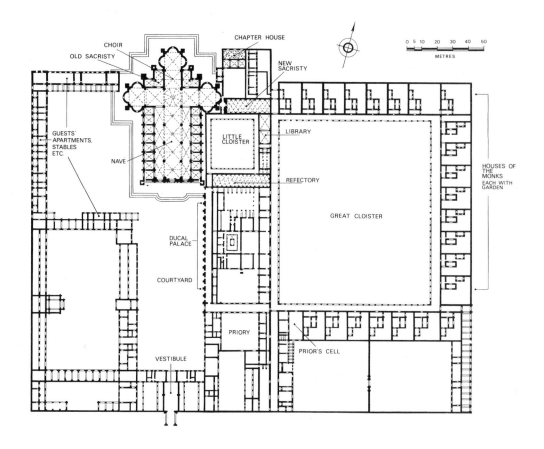

Within the plan:

CHOIR

OLD SACRISTY

CHAPTER HOUSE

NEW SACRISTY

GUESTS' APARTMENTS, STABLES ETC.

NAVE

LITTLE CLOISTER

LIBRARY

REFECTORY

GREAT CLOISTER

HOUSES OF THE MONKS EACH WITH GARDEN

DUCAL PALACE

COURTYARD

PRIORY

PRIOR'S CELL

VESTIBULE

0 5 10 20 30 40 50
METRES

they receive the necessary food for the whole week—bread and vegetables, cooked by each one in his cell; drinking water is supplied by a conduit. . . . They do not go to church for the usual canonical services as we do, but only for certain of them . . . they hardly ever speak, and if they want anything, ask for it by a sign. . . . Lower down the mountain there is a building for about twenty lay brothers who work for them. . . . Although they observe the utmost poverty they are getting together a very rich library.'

Here are already all the essentials of the Carthusian way of life. In place of St Benedict's ideal of a family, sharing everything under the leadership of a paternal abbot, we are faced with a return to a community of hermits, coming together only to ensure their solitude. 124 The first buildings at the Chartreuse must obviously have reflected

A plan of the Certosa, Pavia.

Right, the tomb of Ludovico Sforza, Duke of Milan, and his wife Beatrice d'Este, carved during their lifetime by Cristoforo Solari (1497). The Certosa was the traditional burial place of the Milanese rulers, and the reign of Ludovico, called 'Il Moro' because of his swarthy complexion, marked a period of rapid progress in building. His monument, however, stood originally in Santa Maria delle Grazie, and was only moved to the Certosa in 1564.

this purpose and were repeated in every Carthusian monastery thereafter; the cloister, instead of being a meeting-place leading to the various communal rooms, was simply a passage between the separate cells. The prominent features of Benedictine and Cistercian houses (dormitory, refectory, chapter house, and so on) are insignificant in Carthusian. Their constitution dictates a completely different layout; a Carthusian plan is quite unmistakable.

Bruno wrote no Rule. Like other leaders whom we have met in this book, he had not intended to found a new order. The 'Customs' of the Chartreuse were only written down in 1127 and approved by Innocent II in 1333. In government and relations with the outside world, the Carthusians followed the pattern of the Benedictines. The great difference lay in their internal organisation. Each monk lived in his own little house—it was more than a cell—and in terms of purely physical requirements, a Carthusian monastery is more demanding and more expensive to run than any other. (The Certosa, which is vast, has only 24 houses; even at its peak only 36 professed monks lived there.) The houses were normally of four or five rooms— a storeroom for fuel, a workshop, library and bedroom. Sometimes there was a small antechamber, and usually a garden for growing vegetables. The monk stayed in his house all day, alone. On weekdays he left it only three times, for services in the church (two during the day, one at night). His food was brought in by a lay brother and placed in a *guichet* or hatch beside the cell door, where it was taken in without speaking. At first the food was barely enough to keep alive but this austerity was soon relaxed and meals (two a day) were adequate and well cooked, though Carthusians never did, and never do, eat meat. On Sundays both meals were eaten in common and some conversation was allowed, though it had to be of a serious and improving nature. The lay brothers, whose status was similar to those of the Cistercians, lived the same solitary lives. The Carthusians are remarkable in the history of the monastic orders for never having departed from their original high standards. Their constitution has been subject to minor revisions, but essentially it remains today as St Bruno meant it to be.

The head of the order was the Prior of the Grande Chartreuse, elected by the monks of that house. The priors of the other houses, elected in the same way, submitted to his authority, as the Cluniacs had to the Abbot of Cluny. The order was never as numerous or as powerful as any of those discussed so far. By 1300 there were 39 Carthusian houses, but they increased rather rapidly during the

Above, the door to the Old Sacristy, a splendid work of the late Milanese Renaissance, designed by Amadeo and executed by various hands. Its theme is the two families of Visconti and Sforza united as patrons of the Carthusian order. The three heads at the top are Visconti, while the two pairs below, facing each other, are members of the Sforza family.

Opposite, the Little Cloister. Behind it is the south side of the nave, the crossing tower and the south transept. On the right is part of the plain exterior of the New Sacristy.

127

next century, establishing themselves in most European countries; the name 'Chartreuse' was rendered as 'Charterhouse' in English and as 'Certosa' in Italian.

The Certosa of Pavia is the most splendid and probably the best-known of all Carthusian monasteries apart from the Chartreuse itself. It was founded in 1396 by the Duke of Milan, Giangaleazzo Visconti, one of the most powerful princes of Italy. The site was part of his own estates, belonging to the Castle of Pavia, and the immediate occasion for the foundation was a vow made by his wife Caterina. Later members of the Visconti family and their successors the Sforzas continued to lavish their patronage upon it (indeed it became a sort of ducal Westminster Abbey), a factor which makes it in many ways untypical of the Carthusians, though adding to its interest as a work of art and architecture. The money for its building came from the Milanese court and throughout its subsequent history it lived off the great estates made over to it by Giangaleazzo. Of the priors of the Certosa and of the monks who lived there little has been remembered.

Three leading architects had a hand in the original plans (more are mentioned in the documents; it seems to have been rather a committee affair): Bernardo da Venezia, the master, had already modernised the Castle of Pavia and acted as consultant to the workshop of Milan Cathedral; the second, Giacomo da Campione, was an engineer who had also carried out responsible work for the Visconti; the third, a younger man, was Cristoforo da Conigo, who outlived the other two by many years though he never achieved the senior position. He was later to serve as assistant to Guiniforte Solari and died, aged over 80, in 1460.

The design of the church seems to have been Bernardo's, and although it was changed by later architects it still retains the basically Gothic character that he gave it. By 1412 only the lower walls had been built. In 1428 Giovanni Solari took over, to be succeeded in 1452 by his son, Guiniforte, who under the new dynasty of the Sforzas pushed the work ahead with energy. By 1473 it was complete except for the façade.

The plan is of great interest. Chancel and transepts form three arms, the chancel slightly larger than the other two. All end in a trefoil of apses (see the plan on p. 124), with a pair of narrow square turrets at the corners. The nave proportions are wide, as always with Italian Gothic, and there is little vertical emphasis. The vaulting system is a surprise—it is sexpartite, a form discarded throughout

Right, the Great Cloister. The arcade is decorated in terracotta in the same style as the Little Cloister. In the background are some of the monks' houses that surround it on three sides. Food was passed through the square opening beside each door.

Below right, part of the terracotta decoration on the arcade of the Little Cloister. In the spandrels are busts of prophets and saints, while round the arches and along the frieze lively putti play amid garlands of flowers. Between each trio of putti expressive heads gaze out of medallions.

Far right, one of the houses from the garden side. Two-storeyed and spacious, with a fire for winter (note the unusual chimneys) and an open gallery for summer, these dwellings enabled the Carthusians to lead a life of moderate comfort dedicated to solitude and prayer.

most of Europe in the 12th century; and, even stranger, the subsidiary ribs come down not on to subsidiary piers but on to the keystones of the main arches—structurally, a sound enough idea. Guiniforte Solari, who seems to be the architect responsible, was evidently an engineer of some originality. He supported the nave vault by an aisle vault with oblong bays, and joined its central boss to the aisle with another rib, making it into a lopsided sexpartite bay. It looks less odd in reality than it does on the plan. The thrust of this aisle vault is then carried by a line of vaulted chapels, with exterior buttresses. The aisles at least seem to have been built by Bernardo, though how he intended them to continue it is impossible to say. Probably he meant to have flying buttresses at the next two levels. Guiniforte achieves the same result by two deep exterior loggias, one running along the top of the nave wall, the other along the aisle

The refectory, opposite, is divided into two by a screen wall and two columns—one half for the monks and the other for the lay brothers. To the left, the familiar reader's pulpit. Most meals were eaten alone, but the whole community met on Sundays. The elaborate stalls date from 1621.

Left, the New Sacristy. The room dates originally from the early 15th century, but all decoration is later; much of the painting belongs to the 17th century. Typical of the Certosa's wealth are the wall panels and the presses in the centre for missals and copes.

131

wall—a feature that had been traditional in Lombardy since the 12th century, though never used in quite this way. The nearest parallels are the Cathedral of Milan, begun in 1385 and under construction simultaneously with it, and San Petronio at Bologna, where the arrangement of the vaulting bays, square in the nave and oblong in the aisles, is comparable to the Certosa.

At the crossing rises an octagonal tower diminishing by stages, resting on squinches. Bernardo intended there to be a dome. On the higher parts of the building Renaissance details began to appear everywhere—for instance, while the capitals of the main crossing piers are foliated Gothic, immediately above them, under the squinches, are freely adapted Ionic volutes. The tower itself is a rather unsuccessful compromise, as if the Octagon at Ely had been rebuilt by Sir Christopher Wren. Near by Chiaravalle was the model. Only on the façade does the early Renaissance style take over consistently. This will be described in detail later.

While the great church had been rising, the monastic buildings were going forward on the same lavish scale. The dukes were generous with land: there are two cloisters (one very large), many subsidiary buildings, a wide forecourt, gardens and apartments for guests. Giangaleazzo and his successors regarded the Certosa as a place of retreat and recreation. On one side of the forecourt they built a small palace (as had happened at Poblet) whose façade was designed in the early 17th century by Ricchino, the architect of the Palazzo Brera.

The monks' houses were built in Bernardo's time and temporarily connected by a wooden cloister. The chapter house, library, refectory (used as a chapel until the church was finished) and infirmary date from the period of Giovanni Solari, most of the rest from that of his son Guiniforte. It was during the second half of the 15th century, beginning with the accession of the Sforzas in 1450, that the most striking work was carried out. The two cloisters were both decorated with exquisite terracotta panels and moulded heads. The artist in charge was Rinaldo de Stauris, a woodcarver from Cremona. Other artists employed included the sculptor Antonio Rizzo (who built the Scala dei Giganti in the Doge's Palace at Venice) and the painter Vincenzo Foppa, one of the leaders of the Milanese Renaissance. The first brought costly red *breccia* from Verona, marble and granite for the decoration of the cloisters and doorways; the second painted the walls and vaults in fresco.

The new sacristy and the refectory (redecorated when it reverted

to the use for which it was intended) are so severe and chaste, so 'Florentine' in feeling, that Solari must have come into contact with Tuscan architects or with Antonio Filarete, who was then building the Ospedale Maggiore in Milan in a similar blend of traditional Gothic, classical terracotta and Florentine Renaissance. A certain Benedetto Ferrini of Florence worked at the Certosa in 1469.

The Certosa's great glory is its façade, which has enjoyed a renown perhaps beyond its merits, since it was the first work of the Renaissance to make a really deep impression in France. (The French occupied the Duchy of Milan in 1515, and in fact lost it in a battle just outside Pavia in 1525. During the next ten or twenty years echoes of the Certosa are heard clearly at Blois, Chambord and Fontainebleau.) The style is characteristic of the Lombard Renaissance, though it had rarely been carried to such lengths. Every available inch is filled with figure-sculpture, reliefs or patterns of coloured marble. The details are all classical, but the overall effect is far too rich to evoke plausibly either ancient Rome or 15th-century Florence.

Above left, a detail from the façade—the window to the left of the central door. On the buttresses the statues represent St Andrew, King David, St Peter and St James. Along the bottom are represented scenes and figures from the Old and New Testaments.

Above, the choir stalls, among the glories of the Certosa, were carved between 1487 and 1498, with intarsia panels at the back designed by the Milanese painter Bergognone.

133

The chief name associated with the façade is that of Giovanni Antonio Amadeo, who had been working at the Certosa almost all his life. He is first encountered as a very young man assisting with the terracottas of the cloisters in 1466. Guiniforte Solari certainly made a design for the façade, the only part of the monastery still awaiting completion, but this was thought to be too plain. A new design was commissioned in 1473 from Amadeo in collaboration with others (including the brothers Cristoforo and Antonio Mantegazza) but nothing much seems to have been done. There is evidence for several earlier projects before the present one was agreed upon, and here Amadeo was given a freer hand. Even so, his design was changed halfway through, and the lower part of the façade, completed by him in 1499, is noticeably richer than the upper part, which came later.

The whole façade is a screen concealing rather than expressing the structure behind it. Its main features are the central door and four elaborate windows with carved baluster-mullions (only the inner two are real windows). There are nearly 50 free-standing figures besides the numerous scenes in relief. Their overall theme is the triumph of the Church over paganism, though this is not easy to follow through. Above the central door stand the two founders of the monastery, spiritual and secular, St Bruno and Giangaleazzo Visconti.

In 1499 Amadeo relinquished control and the upper parts were continued by others in a more sober style; it was originally intended to be crowned by a pediment. The main doorway was added in 1501 by Benedetto Briosco. Soon afterwards Erasmus visited the Certosa and wondered why so much money had been spent in building a church destined for the services of a few monks. Montaigne, seeing it in 1581, thought it was more like the palace of a great prince than a monastery.

After the mid-16th century nothing essential was changed or added. Church furnishings, choir stalls and paintings, of which it possesses many, accumulated. In the 17th century the doors of the monks' houses were enlarged and the windows and balustrades rebuilt. Luxury, however, made little difference to the Carthusians. They remained poor amid their wealth, pursuing the even tenor of their way until 1782, when the monastery was suppressed for the first time. They returned in 1843 to a building shorn of much of its splendour, but were finally disbanded in 1881. The Certosa is now a state monument.

The façade of the Certosa, near Pavia, magnificent as it is, expresses rather the structure behind it than the self-denial of the Carthusian monks who lived there. From its foundation in 1396 the church was the family shrine of the Dukes of Milan—first the Visconti, then the Sforzas—who filled it with outstanding works of painting and sculpture. The façade was begun in the lavish Milanese Renaissance style between 1480 and 1499, and finished more soberly during the next century. It was meant to be crowned by a pediment.

CHAPTER 9

SAN CARLO ALLE QUATTRO FONTANE:
THE TRINITARIANS AND BAROQUE

Early in 1634 the Spanish Discalced Trinitarians of Rome decided to rebuild their cramped quarters on the corner of the Via Quattro Fontane and the Via del Quirinale. The commission was given to a young architect of 35 who had never yet designed a major building on his own but whose work under Maderno and Bernini had displayed a highly individual talent, even if his character showed signs of being difficult and morose. It was an adventurous choice and a successful one. The architect was Francesco Borromini, and the building turned out to be one of the masterpieces, some would say *the* masterpiece, of the Roman Baroque.

The Order of Trinitarians had a long and disturbed history. It was founded in 1198 by St John of Matha, a doctor of the University of Paris. Its purpose was a simple and useful one—the ransoming of prisoners from the Muslims. According to its constitution the revenue of this *Ordo Sanctae Trinitas et de redemptione captivorum* was to be divided into three parts—one third for the brethren, one third for the poor and one third to ransom prisoners. Their fund-raising demonstrations and *tableaux vivants* depicting the miseries of the captives at the hands of the Infidel made them popular figures throughout Europe (and perhaps gave them a certain *panache* when it came to choosing their architect). When enough money had been collected, Trinitarian 'ransomers' used to set out to the Barbary Coast (Tunis, Algiers and Morocco), open negotiations with the Moors, choose which prisoners to redeem, fix the price, and arrange for their transport home. It was a delicate and dangerous enterprise, in which many of them lost their lives. In three centuries it is reckoned that they rescued about 90,000 people, including the writer Cervantes (in 1580).

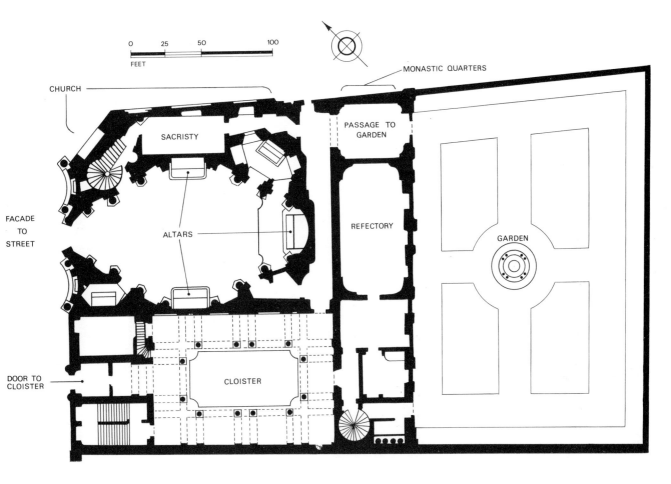

Scale: 0　25　50　100 FEET

MONASTIC QUARTERS

CHURCH

SACRISTY

PASSAGE TO GARDEN

FACADE
TO
STREET

ALTARS

REFECTORY

GARDEN

DOOR TO
CLOISTER

CLOISTER

Towards the end of the 16th century the order split into three, on the usual issue of relaxation of the Rule versus strictness and reform. The Spanish branch, the most austere and dedicated of the three, organised itself under Father Juan Battista of the Immaculate Conception into the Congregation of the Discalced Trinitarians of Spain (discalced means without shoes). They soon spread to Italy; the Convent in Rome was established in 1612, and it was this community that in 1634 became Borromini's patrons.

It was a chance that Borromini had been waiting for. Born in 1599, he had spent the first fifteen years of his working life as a stone-carver and architectural draughtsman to Carlo Maderno, who was a distant relative. In this capacity he had contributed to the nave of St Peter's and to the Palazzo Barberini, two of the major projects

A plan of the monastery of San Carlo alle Quattro Fontane.

137

of contemporary Rome. In 1629 Maderno died and Borromini found himself working under Bernini, whom he grew to dislike intensely. To a man of Borromini's temperament (reserved, neurotic, conscientious to the point of mania) Bernini's easy success—he was only a year older than Borromini—and aristocratic manner must have been hard to bear. His grudge developed into a gnawing jealousy that remained with him all his life. Bernini, on the other hand, seems to have been favourably impressed by Borromini's talents and was ready to give him considerable responsibility. The top storey of the Palazzo Barberini is largely Borromini's work and the first example of his own expressive style. Going beyond the innovations of the later Mannerists, he broke more rules and achieved more exciting results than any architect since Michelangelo—the only master, apart from Maderno, to whom he admitted that he owed anything. All Borromini's intense and frustrated energy poured into his architecture, and the style he created—brilliant, idiosyncratic, sometimes perverse, always minutely and consistently detailed—expressed the man. He was incapable of compromise. His clients sometimes got more than they bargained for, but for those sensitive to his genius the appeal must have been irresistible. Father Giovanni della Annunziatione, Procurator-General of the Congregation in Rome, took the risk.

The scale of San Carlo is completely different from anything we have so far considered. It is a monastery in miniature (hence its diminutive nickname of *San Carlino*) and presented Borromini with a major problem of planning before he could even begin. The site is an irregular rectangle at the corner of a busy crossroads (each of the four streets has a fountain—the *Quattro Fontane*). His first task was to provide living accommodation for the brothers; then they needed a cloister and finally a church. He divided the available area into three. A long block, fronting the street only at one of the narrow ends, occupied the middle. This was the convent proper. On one side, furthest from the traffic, he put the garden; on the other, the church and cloister.

Work on the conventual building began in July 1634 and took just over a year. The monks moved in in August 1635. On the ground floor were the service rooms, passages to the garden, the kitchen and the refectory—the last a large room (in San Carlino terms) on the axis of the church (then unbuilt) but at right angles to it. It is lit by three windows looking on to the garden. At one end is a shallow niche made to appear deeper by perspective mouldings and the

The monastery of San Carlo alle Quattro Fontane stands on a busy crossroads in Rome (one of its 'four fountains' can be seen in the foreground) and is on so small a scale that it has been calculated that the whole church would fit inside one of the crossing piers of St Peter's. Francesco Borromini, however, made it a landmark in architectural history by his manipulation of space and dynamic treatment of surfaces and volumes. The façade, his last work (begun 1665), is very much in his personal style—concave and convex playing a subtle counterpoint, while the columns, cornices and ornament accentuate and prolong the rhythm. Behind the façade can be seen the lantern of the dome, and to its left the bell-tower—both of them further exercises in the interplay of curving forms.

corners are rounded. A coved ceiling rises from the gentle curves of the walls ('the corner' said Borromini, 'is the enemy of all good architecture'). This room formerly contained a pulpit for the meal-time readings, but in the early 18th century it was converted into a sacristy when another larger refectory was built in what used to be the garden.

On the floor above the refectory are the brethren's cells—two rows of small rooms without distinctive features. The top floor has again been changed since Borromini's time. Loggias were built out and the proportions altered. Borromini's original designs for the garden front show how deliberately he had articulated the building, making the exterior an expression of the inner organisation. At the top and bottom are the large windows and enriched panelling of the

Above left, the urban monastery, San Carlo, squeezed between the city blocks of modern Rome. The central lantern of the church stands out at the corner of the crossroads (from this vantage point, its similarity to a late Roman temple like that of Venus at Baalbek is particularly striking), and to its right one gets a glimpse of the cloister. Of the U-shaped block behind it, only the side nearest the church is original.

refectory and library; in between come the stark, undecorated square windows of the cells. Many of the details on this side are characteristic of Borromini's work; the pediment on the roof belongs to a type developed from Michelangelo's Porta Pia and used by Borromini extensively in later buildings. The doorway, with its dynamic projections and recessions and its tense lines, is similar to those he invented for the Palazzo Barberini.

Next came the cloister. This was begun in February 1635 and finished in October 1644. Remembering the cloisters we have seen so far in this book, that of San Cárlo comes as something of a shock. Two bays long and one bay wide, its cramped proportions seem only to be intensified by its height of two storeys. It is in fact a good deal higher than it is wide, but Borromini makes a virtue of necessity

Left, the cloister of San Carlo, looking from the entrance passage towards the convent. The style is deliberately plain and massive, Borromini's characteristic subtleties appearing only in such features as the convex corners and the rhythmic balustrade of the gallery.

by manipulating the volumes in a way that gives every part an interest of its own. The simply moulded arches are supported by plain Tuscan columns. Each arch rests on its own pair of columns, so that the arcade is not continuous and each pair of adjacent columns shares an elongated capital with a square panel of masonry above it. The effect is deliberately massive and seems to be adapted from a traditional Lombard scheme: perhaps Borromini was remembering Lake Lugano where he was born. At the corners, however (and this is very typical of him), the space between the columns is convex, its curve echoing the bulging columns beside it. The balustrade above again echoes the shape of the wall, providing a miniature counterpoint of its own by means of triangular balusters bulging alternately at the top and bottom. Above the second level of columns is a straight entablature.

The church, the last and most carefully considered part of the monastery, was begun in 1638. Borromini took immense pains over it. Several projects, often worked out in great detail, were discarded before he arrived at his final version. To understand it one has to analyse it geometrically, constructing it as Borromini did. The experience, however, when one is actually inside it, is immediate. One is not aware how the effect is achieved; one only knows that highly complicated spaces are flowing into one another and forming a unity—that niches, panels, columns, curving and straight entablatures, concave pediments, stucco medallions and the receding coffers of the oval dome are all part of one dynamic movement.

Borromini, one has to remember, was in some ways an old-fashioned architect. He learnt his trade as a stone-cutter and his instincts were those of a medieval master-mason rather than of a disciple of Vitruvius and Alberti. He began by constructing his plan in terms of triangles, working out the proportions geometrically (mostly as subdivisions of the triangle or figures derived from it) unlike more classically-minded designers who used a module based on the diameter of the column. In his later church of Sant' Ivo the basic form—two interlocking triangles forming a six-pointed star— is immediately apparent. At San Carlo it is more complex. Two equilateral triangles are placed base to base, forming a rhomboid. Intersecting circles are then drawn, touching the corners of the triangles. From the points of the intersection other circles are described with various related radii and the adjoining segments joined together. The result is a complicated but regular shape, the sides undulating

Opposite, Borromini's design for the front facing the garden—a four-storey elevation clearly reflecting the division of parts behind. The ground floor has doorways at each end and seven windows (one of them blank), in reality almost equal in size though made to look alternately large and small by the framing round them. The next two floors are the monastic cells. For the top storey he made two alternative elevations (both seen here), one elaborating the three large windows of the library, the other placing the emphasis on a high upper feature with an ogee pediment. The curly aedicules above the roof line were terracotta chimneys.

143

Above, looking down from the vault—a dramatic view that captures the brilliance of Borromini's plan and and the spatial interplay that it achieves.

This door, left, opens from the street into the passage leading straight into the cloister. Typical of Borromini are the raising of the whole semicircular pediment on consoles, the turning of the sides at an angle so that they project into another dimension, and the use of sculpture (a cherub with four wings) to add movement to the architectural forms.

but controlled, combining two types of plan that were proving particularly fascinating to contemporary architects—the Greek cross and the oval. Upon this outline Borromini now places his major accents—16 large 'Ionic' columns (with the volutes turning up instead of down) and upon the columns a cornice whose shape follows the original lines of the composition: almost a semicircle in the east and west; a semi-oval on the north and south; and in between, sections of straight entablature—small sections, in fact, of the original double triangle. The narrow curves of the east and west incorporate the entrance and the altar and the flatter curves subsidiary altars, while the sections of straight entablature become 'piers' to support the pendentives for the oval dome. The dome itself, with its very busy coffered surface based on a Roman mosaic, rises to an oval lantern where within a circle shines the triangle of the Trinity—a neat summing up of both Christian theology and architecture.

Above, the crypt of San Carlo. Shorn of its columns, entablature and decoration, this is the elementary shape of the church above. Here was the brethren's burial place and here Borromini intended his own tomb.

145

The design, for all its subtlety, is extremely practical. The 'straight' sections contain four doors. One leads out of the church towards the cloister, one to a staircase, the other two to tiny sacristies fitted into the odd spaces that happened to be available. San Carlo is an extraordinary achievement, so complex that it exhausts analysis and yet finally so simple and so exhilarating. Underneath the church is a crypt in which, with even greater simplicity, the lines of the walls (alternately straight and curved) are carried directly up into the vault—an idea that Borromini was to use on a large scale at Sant' Ivo.

The façade remained unfinished for nearly thirty years. In 1665 Borromini, now an elderly man, successful enough but disappointed in many of his most ambitious projects, came back to San Carlo to build it. It was not finished until after his death and we cannot be quite sure that the upper part is in accordance with his wishes. But its main accents are unmistakably his. It consists of a framework of eight giant columns, four standing on four. Between them the surface undulates in a play of curves, as does the interior: on the ground floor concave–convex–concave; on the upper storey concave–

Two views of the interior: left, looking towards the high altar, and above, towards the altar on the right. The tall columns with their inverted Ionic volutes and uninterrupted entablature define the basic structure. Threading through them are two more horizontal courses, one corresponding to the lintels of the doors, the other to the springing of the arches over the altars and larger niches. The wall surface comes forward between the columns and recedes behind them.

147

concave–concave. In the middle section of the upper storey a convex
motif is supplied by a small '*tempietto*' containing a window; an
allusion, probably, to some late Roman building. Above this is an
oval medallion carried by angels and containing originally a painting
of San Carlo Borromeo. Can Borromini have intended this very
uncharacteristic and unarchitectural feature? It is at least possible
that he planned to link interior and exterior at this point by a window
148 looking down through the façade of the church, but had failed to

*The dome of the church, looking up into the
lantern. The pattern of coffers—octagons,
elongated hexagons and crosses—was taken
from the late Roman church of Santa Costanza
in Rome. There, however, they formed a barrel-
vault. Here, by being adapted to an oval and
diminishing in size towards the centre, they give
an impression of increased height. Two of the
octagons were intended as windows.*

work it out in detail. Sculptured enrichment is freely used—most strikingly in the figure of San Carlo himself over the central door, where the frame of the niche is formed by the wings of angels.

It is pleasant to know that the Trinitarians appreciated Borromini's achievement. There is a glowing description of 'this marvellous convent' written soon after it was finished by the then Procurator-General, Frate Juan de San Bonaventura. He gives many details of its history, listing all the rooms and services that Borromini had provided—garden, refectory, dormitory, cloister, kitchen, running water, latrines, servants' quarters, library, staircases, infirmary, entrance lodge, cellars, church (with a crypt for burials), sacristy, chapels—'everything as the Procurator-General had asked'. And he concludes with these very perceptive remarks:

> 'Many who have visited it can hardly believe that it is all contained in the building which they see from outside. . . . To arrange it all on this cramped and irregular site Messer Francesco needed to use all his wit: it is an extraordinary design which owes nothing to any other architect. Yet it is based on the antique, and conforms to what the greatest architects have written. Everyone agrees that it is first in composition and in skill and that nowhere can anything like it be found for brilliance, caprice, singularity and novelty in the whole world. This is proved by the fact that people are continually coming to Rome to try and get the plans. . . . All the parts [of the church] are arranged in such a way that one seems to echo another, each one leading the spectator on to look at the next. Many times, looking down from the *tribuna* or the lattice-screen of the church, we have seen visitors acting just like this, unable either to tear themselves away or to say a word for a long time. . . . It seems to me that this work has in it something of the imitation of the Divine—*qualche cosa di imitazione di Divinità*.'

While the façade was being built Borromini committed suicide. He was ill and suffering from acute depression. His final act is said to have been caused by being refused a light to read by. Some time earlier he had given a large donation to the Trinitarians and received permission to build himself a chapel in the crypt. But he was not buried at San Carlo. As he lay dying he asked that his body should be placed in the tomb of Carlo Maderno and that there should be no inscription.

The façade elevation, from a book of engravings published in 1684. Only the two main storeys can be seen from the street, the lantern of the dome, prominent here, being completely hidden. 149

Above, a longitudinal section through the church, the façade on the left, the high altar on the right, from the same book of engravings. Here both the octagonal windows in the vault are clearly shown.

Left, the undulating façade as it looks today. In spite of its complexity, the composition is unified partly by its iconographic programme. Dedicated, as the inscription tells us, to the Holy Trinity and to San Carlo Borromeo, the repeated threefold rhythm leads our eye to the figure of San Carlo himself, who, framed by the wings of seraphim (one looking towards him and one away, a particularly Borrominesque touch), gazes upward with a rapt expression.

CHAPTER 10

OTTOBEUREN:
THE 18TH CENTURY IN CENTRAL EUROPE

Germany in the 18th century was a prosperous and agreeable country. Divided politically into innumerable dukedoms and principalities and religiously into a Protestant north and a Catholic south, it had nevertheless made one of those spectacular economic recoveries from the ravages of war with which we are familiar in the present century. The Thirty Years War had been a time of immense suffering in large areas of Central Europe. Now, with peace, the people were eager to restore their agriculture and commerce, the rulers to revive the splendid manner of life that was again within their reach, and the Church, one of the greatest landowners in Germany, to reap once more the benefits of secure rents and stable patronage.

These conditions alone would not account for the great wave of church and monastery building that swept across Austria and Bavaria in the 18th century. There was also an ideological cause. The religious conflict that had begun with Luther had not ended. It was only transposed from armed conflict to the battle of ideas, the south looking towards the Hapsburg Empire and the Mediterranean, the north cultivating its own austere political and religious code. In music and philosophy the honours perhaps lie with the north; in architecture the south is undeniably the more fertile and interesting.

The Counter Reformation gave Baroque architecture in Germany both its impetus and much of its character. It is a committed and didactic art. The appeal to the senses, abjured in the north, is ecstatically and deliberately exploited in the south. Every device is used: colour, form, symbolism and drama—all are raised to an emotional pitch such as had rarely been attempted in Western architecture before. The message to be conveyed is a joyful one;

these are certainly the gayest churches ever built. In sculpture, *putti* dance, angels rejoice, saints stretch out their arms in welcome. In painting Christ blesses, the Virgin intercedes and protects, the triumphant army of the saved are received into the bliss of heaven. Too theatrical? It is theatrical to this extent: that it makes a conscious attempt to draw the onlooker inside and to move him emotionally when he is there. These churches are not simply buildings in which worship takes place, but themselves expressions of that worship, in the same explicit sense as paintings or statues are. That is part of their excitement. To one who resists the excitement (in other words, anyone who insists on looking at them from a purely 'architectural' point of view) they appear excessive and contrived. But just as the austerity of the 12th-century Cistercian style may legitimately demand some imaginative effort, so in the opposite way may 18th-century Baroque.

An analysis of the style reveals a fusion of influences from France and Italy. From Italy comes the love of complicated geometry and the moulding of internal space; from France the graceful ornament hitherto used on a small scale in furniture and interior decoration, but now incorporated into architecture. The result is a new freedom, in which classical features like columns, pilasters, arches, keystones, pediments and entablatures cease to have any relation to function. They are used to define the spaces and volume by suggesting structure without depending on it. Walls undulate, capitals erupt into the ceiling, arches leap into impossible arabesques. This is achieved by building not in stone but in wood and stucco. The darker accents are the heavy columns of imitation marble (red, green, blue, mottled into a richness unknown to geology); the lighter are the gilding, the elaborate wrought-iron work and the woodcarving. The walls are always pure white. Statues echo the lines of the building with exuberant gestures and swirling draperies. Painting is normally confined to the vault and to altar panels, but these often overlap their frames, two dimensions flowing imperceptibly into three. Each part is as organically related to the whole as a single line of music is to the complete harmony. To take one Baroque statue and put it into a museum is like playing the cello part of a Mozart symphony on its own.

It was providential that the architects available included so many of genius. In the front rank are Balthazar Neumann, Fischer von Erlach, Dominikus Zimmermann, the brothers Asam and Johann Michael Fischer, the designer of Ottobeuren. Monastic churches

Two examples of the great wave of monastic building that took place in Germany and Austria during the 18th century: Weingarten (above), a Benedictine abbey, was rebuilt between 1714 and 1724 by Casper Moosbrugger. Melk (left), towering above the Danube, is the masterpiece of Jakob Prandtauer.

Overleaf, the ceiling of Zweifalten, another church by Johann Michael Fischer, the architect of Ottobeuren. The painting is by Spiegler and shows the human race (at the bottom and sides) led by St Benedict, in ecstatic adoration before the Virgin and Child. It is typical of the religious art of the time. Painting overflows into the stucco-work and seems to transform even the architecture into a hymn of praise. 153

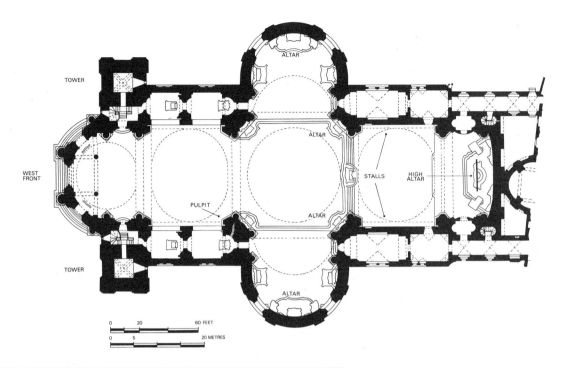

Above, a plan of the abbey church of Ottobeuren.

Left, the library of Metten, one of the most exciting of the new monastic libraries. The ceiling rests on dancing Atlas figures and the whole conception abounds in movement and colour.

Perhaps the most surprising feature of any south German monastery of this period is the pulpit, opposite, at Irsee—an extravagant jeu d'esprit in the shape of a ship's prow, complete with sail, mast, rigging (in which putti clamber energetically) and, on the other side, an anchor. The figurehead is St Michael.

oddly enough, are at least as uninhibited as the rest. And not only the churches. The chapter houses and libraries too are so full of colour and movement that one wonders how the monks could ever concentrate in them. The Jesuits had always made a point of providing exciting churches, lavish services and sumptuous music; they were out for converts. But in south Germany the Jesuits were far outshone by the Benedictines and the Augustinians, and even by the Cistercians.

The Benedictine abbey of Ottobeuren was founded, according to the chronicles, in 764. Charlemagne endowed it with extensive estates. Some of the abbots were important figures, including a saint, Ulrich, who became Bishop of Augsburg. At the beginning of the 18th century the monastery buildings were a mixture of various dates, some parts dating back to the early 13th century, others as recent as 1564. Fragments of Gothic sculpture from it are preserved in the abbey museum.

In 1710 an extremely energetic new abbot took over—Rupert von Wangen. He represents the spirit of renewal and progress at Ottobeuren and he seems to have been one of those men, like Louis XIV or Ludwig II, with a natural passion for building. He decided to demolish and rebuild the entire monastery, and during his thirty years of office (he died in 1740) his ambition was almost completely fulfilled, though, ironically, he never lived to see the great glory of the new Ottobeuren, its church.

For the layout of the monastic buildings the old Benedictine plan was abandoned. Ottobeuren bears more resemblance to a palace or *Residenz* than to the traditional abbey. The plan is a grid of four wings forming a square divided by a cross in the centre (one arm of the cross was omitted in the building, thus throwing two of the four small courts into one large one). It was drawn up by Father Christoph Vogt, the father-confessor of Ottobeuren, but a man of considerable architectural experience too. (He also supplied a plan of the church, which was not used, but its model—Fischer von Erlach's Kollegienkirche at Salzburg—continued to influence the church that was eventually built.) The foundation stone was laid in 1711. In 1717 the architect Simpert Kramer was called in and in 1728 another, Andrea Maini. Kramer was a mason from the Allgau who had already worked on several monasteries in south Germany. Maini was primarily a stucco-artist and came from Lugano. The various parts of the abbey were built in the following sequence: the east wing in 1715; next the north, south and central wings; then the west

Opposite, Ottobeuren from the air. From the outside, Ottobeuren seems very like a secular palace, and the church, instead of being absorbed in the monastery, stands proudly isolated.

Left, the centre of one of the wings. Ornament is completely absent except round the door, but there is considerable geometrical play between flat, concave and convex surfaces.

Below, a corridor, with cells opening from it. This is as close as Ottobeuren comes to the traditional cloister.

wing in 1719–25. This was fast work. The interior decoration took a good deal longer, and with reason. For while the exteriors are on the whole plain and modest (except for raised pavilions at the corners) the interiors can vie in richness with any secular palace. Among the artists employed on it were Johann Baptist Zimmermann (the brother of Dominikus, the architect, and a stucco-artist of great ability), Christoph Zopf, Karl Radmüller and Johann Michael Feuchtmayer. All were outstanding stuccoists (that is, they made both statues and ornament in plaster), though Feuchtmayer was perhaps the greatest.

The number, size and luxury of the apartments at Ottobeuren are astonishing. Stuccoed and painted corridors and staircases lead from room to room, each more splendid than the last. In the east wing is the chapter house, its ceiling carried (or apparently carried) on huge imitation-marble columns. The library has 44 of these columns supporting a gallery; the woodwork, panelling and gilding are of the highest quality (matched indeed by the books themselves, for this was the great age of fine printing and binding). Most magnificent of all is the *Kaisersaal*, a great hall with carved and gilded figures of the Hapsburg emperors by the Füssen artist Johann Anton Stürm.

The church surpasses everything else. Its position is unusual, projecting from the north side of the monastery and visible from all sides except the chancel end. Abbot Rupert began commissioning plans for it during the 1730s, but seems to have suffered from a

Opposite top, the library—less eccentric than the one at Metten but equally rich. The gallery is supported on pillars of imitation marble, matched by pilasters on each side of the bookcases. On the ceiling allegories of learning are framed by graceful stucco cartouches.

Many of the leading monasteries were provided with a Kaisersaal, a grand hall in which to receive the emperor, should he ever pay a visit. The one at Ottobeuren, opposite bottom, is a fine example. At the bases of the columns stand gilded statues of the Hapsburg emperors by Anton Sturm. Note too the highly inventive ceiling with stucco figures perched on a pseudo-balustrade.

Left, the exterior of the church, completed by Johann Michael Fischer in 1766. Where an Italian, French or English architect would have placed a dome, Fischer uses only a shallow pyramid. The towers give the only emphasis to an otherwise restrained design.

Far left, looking back towards the entrance wall. On the right the transept opens off, but is united to the body of the nave by the curved crossing-pier, a device of Fischer's which was not part of the original plan.

Centre, the pulpit. This is German Baroque at its most exuberant. The whole pulpit seems to be floating on the clouds, borne on the same spiritual breeze as that which carries the Virgin in the realistic Assumption above.

Left, the interior, looking towards the altar. The church is vaulted with three saucer-domes. We are standing under the first; the next covers the crossing and the third the choir.

The choir stalls and organ, below, contain carving of amazing virtuosity. Every detail of this superb interior is worth study, not least for the successful way it shares in the total design.

superfluity of architects. Three detailed designs were made: by Maini (1731), Dominikus Zimmermann (1732) and Simpert Kramer (1736). Zimmermann's was the most interesting, with an oval central space as at Steinhausen, but it was Kramer's that was finally chosen. He replaced the oval by the more traditional cruciform plan, with the transepts ending in apses. Work began in 1737 but progressed slowly. Rupert died in 1740 and his successor, Anselm Erb, had Kramer's design revised by Joseph Effner, the Bavarian court architect. Finally in 1748 came the man who above all others was to leave the stamp of his own genius at Ottobeuren, Johann Michael Fischer.

Fischer faced the apparently thankless task of completing a church whose main features had already been decided. But he managed to achieve a result intensely his own by modifying the plan as far as he could and redesigning the whole of the elevation and vaulting. The cruciform plan had to be retained, but he chamfered the crossing piers, thus giving the church a more centralised appearance; he further united the parts by giving up the idea of a central dome on a drum and covering all three sections (nave, crossing and chancel) with saucer or hemispherical vaults. The body of the church, which is made of brick, was finished in 1756; four years later the towers were built and the whole was consecrated in 1766, just two years late for the 1000th anniversary of its foundation.

In its structure the church, which is still basically basilican, follows Fischer's favourite method of buttressing by means of integrated chapels instead of aisles. His renunciation of a high dome left him freer in his arrangement of the interior, and he combines clarity of parts with all-over unity in a most masterly way. Alternating columns and pilasters help to define the basic elements and the fluctuating projections and recessions of the tall entablature that they carry also have their own quite consistent logic. The altar dominates by its size and splendour and by the fact that only here do the restless curves come to rest in a flat surface.

In this kind of building it is impossible to separate the effect of the architecture from that of the decoration. At Ottobeuren this was in the hands of Johann Michael Feuchtmayer, the stuccoist, and Johann Jakob Zeiller, who painted the frescoes and altar panels. The theme of the nave is the triumph of the Benedictine Order, that of the crossing the working of salvation through the Holy Spirit (in the transepts the Virgin and martyrs) and of the chancel the Last Judgement. The whole choir (this is again typical of German Baroque) is organised round a single theme that governs both the subject-matter, the symbolism and the decoration; here it centres on Zeiller's *Trinity*, with sculptured figures of St Peter and St Paul and local saints in adoration before it. All the altars in the church are by Joseph Christian, a sculptor who had already collaborated with Fischer and Feuchtmayer at Zweifelten. The choir stalls, organ-case and pulpits, also carefully integrated with the whole composition, are by Christian and others. All the furniture and decoration at Ottobeuren is of the very highest quality.

The façade, the last part to be completed, has something of the same dynamic movement as the interior without its lavishness. The convex front between two square towers was a legacy from the earlier plans. Fischer elaborated it in a style he had used earlier for other of his churches. The most notable features are the very lively curved pediment, the straight-sided 'onion domes' of the towers and the subtle arrangement of the corners, which are chamfered but at the same time emphasised by means of overlapping pilasters. The figure in the central niche is St Bernard, the others various early benefactors of the abbey.

Ottobeuren was secularised for a short time in the 19th century but is now again a working Benedictine foundation. It was not damaged in either war and is in perfect condition.

The Baroque churches of south Germany, of which Ottobeuren is one of the most splendid, are true products of the union of all the arts. The flowing spaces conceived by Johann Michael Fischer are re-interpreted in their own media by his stuccoists, carpenters and painters. Veined columns against pure white walls spell out the geometrical scheme; golden acanthus leaves lap round the meeting of planes; groups of ecstatic angels rise at key points such as the springing of arches; and the shallow domes, transformed into vistas of the supernatural, beckon the worshipper towards the drama of the high altar.

CHAPTER 11

CLEWER:
VICTORIAN REVIVAL

Monasticism, the Catholic religion and Gothic architecture all ended together in England in the reign of Henry VIII; they all revived together in that of Queen Victoria. This deliberately provocative statement serves to bring out a connection of some interest. Catholicism and Gothic, of course, had both persisted in underprivileged positions throughout the 17th and 18th centuries. Catholics were excluded from public office and from many of the professions until the Emancipation Act of 1829. By 1850 they had a fully organised hierarchy complete with cardinal. More significant, however, than this official recognition, which was mainly the effect of growing religious toleration, was the revival of old forms of worship within the Church of England. The High Church party felt the need (partly in order to dissociate itself from Nonconformity) to order their services in the old way—to establish, in fact, Henry VIII's ideal of a Church Catholic in everything except submission to the pope. The clearest manifestations were the Tractarians or Oxford Movement (begun in 1833), and the Cambridge Camden Society (founded in 1839).

The story of the Gothic Revival in architecture is closely bound up with these developments. Traditional liturgy and vestments called for a traditional setting. Gothic, which had been one of many historical styles with which architects amused themselves, became the only style for churches. Altars went back against the east wall; chancels were lengthened to accommodate choirs; screens again separated the priest from his congregation. Both strands come together in the compelling figure of Augustus Northmore Welby Pugin, a single-minded lover of the middle ages who was converted to Roman Catholicism chiefly because of his devotion to the Gothic

A contemporary drawing, a view from the south, showing the convent at the time when the first buildings were already standing and the second stage planned.

style. Pugin set himself, in his architectural practice and in his numerous books and pamphlets, to prove that the Gothic or 'Pointed' style was the true 'Christian' style, and that everything else was pagan, commercial or ridiculous. His influence was profound. Almost all the architects of the next generation strove with a mixture of personal passion and historical exactitude to make Gothic express the ideals, aspirations and achievements of Victorian England.

In such an atmosphere it was natural enough that the monastic life should be seriously re-examined. Pugin himself, towards the end of his short life, built a house for himself at Ramsgate with a church *and a monastery* attached, all at his own expense. While the first Anglican Benedictine houses did not come until the second

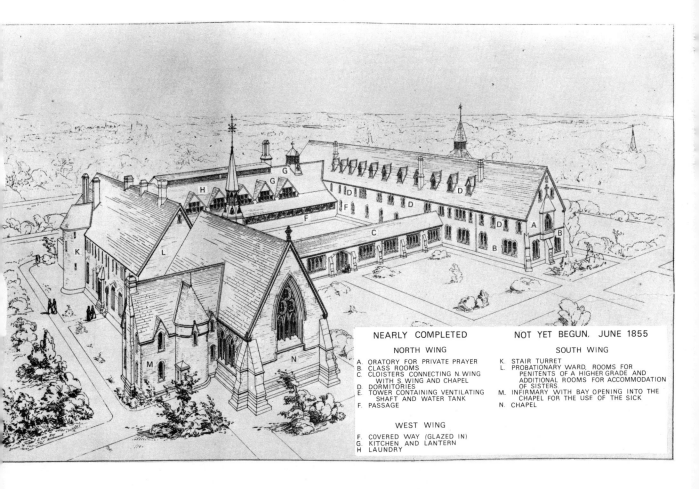

NEARLY COMPLETED

NORTH WING

A. ORATORY FOR PRIVATE PRAYER
B. CLASS ROOMS
C. CLOISTERS CONNECTING N. WING WITH S. WING AND CHAPEL
D. DORMITORIES
E. TOWER CONTAINING VENTILATING SHAFT AND WATER TANK
F. PASSAGE

WEST WING

F. COVERED WAY (GLAZED IN)
G. KITCHEN AND LANTERN
H. LAUNDRY

NOT YET BEGUN. JUNE 1855

SOUTH WING

K. STAIR TURRET
L. PROBATIONARY WARD. ROOMS FOR PENITENTS OF A HIGHER GRADE AND ADDITIONAL ROOMS FOR ACCOMMODATION OF SISTERS.
M. INFIRMARY WITH BAY OPENING INTO THE CHAPEL FOR THE USE OF THE SICK
N. CHAPEL

Left, a view of Clewer from the roof of the new chapel, taken from almost the same point as that of the drawing on p. 165. The dormitory block, in the centre, is unchanged apart from the flat-roofed addition at one end. Behind it can be seen the pyramid roof staircase-tower. To the left is the low east cloister walk and beyond that the west range with laundry and kitchen; the former has been heightened, losing its interesting louvre roof.

Below, a continuation of the view above showing, to the right, later buildings of the sixties and seventies.

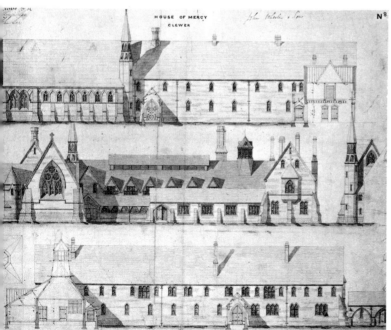

HOUSE OF MERCY
CLEWER

Above, the old courtyard looking north-west. The low roof in the centre marks the kitchen, now sadly deprived of its lantern. On the right is the block where the girls lived, with the dormitory at the top.

Left, drawings prepared by John Wheeler and Sons, the builders, for the first quadrangle at Clewer in 1854. At the top is the south side, with the early chapel, then (in section) the east cloister walk, the sisters' wing and (again in section) the slightly lower west wing with its glazed corridor. The middle drawing shows the western elevation: the east end of the old chapel, the laundry and kitchen (in front of it—shown broken off half-way—the east cloister) and east gable of the dormitory block. At the bottom is the penitents' wing, with the kitchen in section (diagram of the roof); for some curious reason the dormer windows are not included.

167

half of the century, the first woman to take religious vows in England since the Dissolution did so in 1841. Typically, though, a Victorian nunnery was not seen as a retreat from the world for contemplation, but as an institution for performing some useful task. The first nuns were nurses. A similar mission was to be the origin of the sisterhood of Clewer.

Clewer in the 1850s was a rough, working-class suburb of Windsor, 'a mere hamlet, in which besides some respectable cottages, there was a group of as wretched hovels as could be found anywhere in England and inhabited by as wretched a set of abandoned women'. One of the prostitutes there, trying to escape from her way of life, went to see the curate. He sent her to a widow living near by, a Mrs Tennant (she was Spanish but had married an English clergyman) who agreed to take her into her home. Others soon came, and within three months there were 18 girls—more than Mrs Tennant could manage.

At this point enters the presiding personality of Clewer—the rector, Thomas Thellusen Carter (whose description of it we have just quoted). He was then a man in his early 40s, of great zeal and initiative but also with strong spiritual leanings (as his bishop put it, 'Mr Carter is often *upstairs*'). He was the author of voluminous tracts and books of moral exhortation, written in a tone that is today found somewhat suffocating. He was a staunch High Churchman and, in spite of his popularity and evident talents, was eventually compelled to resign because of his insistence on the wearing of full vestments during services.

Carter threw himself into the work of reforming the prostitutes of Clewer with his usual energy. He decided that the normal methods of dealing with the problem were inadequate and that the only hope of success lay with a sisterhood of voluntary workers—'that, instead of being a paid service,' as he wrote, 'it should be carried on as a religious work for Christ's sake.' To lead it he found a remarkable woman, Harriet Monsell, also recently widowed. On St Andrew's Day, 1852, she made her profession and was appointed Mother Superior of the House of Mercy at Clewer by the Bishop of Oxford. The Rule of the order was not written down until 1863 and was kept deliberately flexible. The only condition was that all members had to be practising Anglicans. They took no vows and were free to leave at any time, though it was made clear that profession was meant to be for life.

Permanent quarters for the order were begun in 1854 and the

Below, the orphanage, built in 1858 as St John's Home (now St Anne's House), about 100 yards north of the convent. Typical of Woodyer are the fantastic chimneys—now threatened with demolition—and the painfully sharp angles of the gables: the outline of a now vanished steep-gabled porch can be seen over the door.

architect was Henry Woodyer of Guildford. Woodyer was a pupil of William Butterfield, the architect of All Saints, Margaret Street, and Keble College, Oxford, and therefore in the mainstream of Puginesque inspiration. He had a successful practice in the Home Counties, building churches, hospitals and schools in Berkshire, Hampshire, Surrey and Sussex, but achieving no more than a local reputation. He built only one church in London and rarely published in the architectural magazines. Little is known of his life and even the circumstances of his connection with Clewer are still largely a mystery. He charged no fee for over thirty years of hard, though intermittent, work, so must clearly have been involved personally. Yet he is hardly mentioned in Carter's published account and letters and seems not to have been a close friend of either Carter or Mother Monsell. It is nevertheless to him that Clewer owes so much of its character today.

The House of Mercy was built in stages between 1855 and 1881, but the whole project was fairly clearly thought out from the start. The first stage was a wing to hold 75 'penitents' besides the sisters. It had to contain a classroom, kitchen, laundry and other offices and a dormitory, which took up the whole of the upper

The corridor, west wing. The use of plain brick, timber and small leaded lights shows the influence of English vernacular architecture and points forward to the early 20th. century. The cheerfulness of this corridor must have been somewhat less when the walls were painted brown and decorated with Biblical texts.

169

floor. This long room was converted into a chapel for the dedication ceremony, at which the Bishop of Oxford preached a sermon on the healing of the leper. By 1858 two more wings had been added, including better rooms for the sisters and a chapel.

In accordance with the moral feelings of the age, the girls' period of education and reformation was not made unduly pleasant. 'Penitents' they were called, and Clewer was a 'penitentiary', a word that has become synonymous with prison. They were never left alone. Every minute of the day was occupied with lessons, the kitchen, the laundry and needlework. Their dormitory was divided into compartments of four beds each, with the sisters' rooms interspersed and windows in the partitions. No door could be locked. Even in the passages there were mirrors fixed to the wall at certain points so that a sister stationed in an upper room could keep watch. 'No one', comments the High Church magazine *The Ecclesiologist*, 'who has been taught as a child how a certain man was overtaken and slain by the enemy because a certain horse lacked a nail to a certain shoe, will despise these details.' They were taught

Above, the west front and, above right, the east end of the new chapel of 1881. Basically simple in design, the chapel is enriched with carving and colour. The roof is of grey slate, the bell-turret of lead, the door and window surrounds of red sandstone. The division into nave and chancel is reflected in the different roof spans.

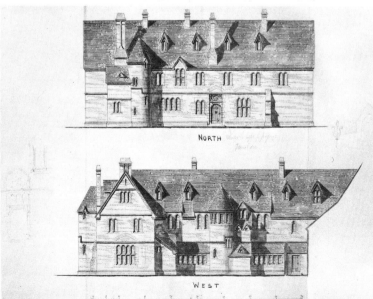

Left, Wheelers' drawings for the extensions of 1872. A note under the door in the upper drawings says, 'Must be light for passage. Panel over'; and on the left, faintly sketched, is what seems to be Woodyer's suggested solution.

NORTH

WEST

a useful occupation and found work. Their usual stay was a year and a half and they were not let out until Carter was convinced that they were reformed and 'settled communicants' of the Church of England.

Woodyer's buildings are an admirable example of what architects meant by calling Gothic 'practical'. For instead of having to torture all their buildings into an artificial classical symmetry, they were able to let each part express its function without disguise, no matter how irregular the result (in fact the more irregular the better). Woodyer exploited the picturesque effects thus produced to the fullest advantage, adding to them touches of inventive eccentricity that no pupil of Butterfield could be expected to forgo. The main group surrounds a square courtyard, with wings projecting beyond it wherever necessary. The north wing, with the dormitory, has dormer windows with Woodyer's typically spiky tops. The west, facing the road, contained the laundry (lit by large gable windows and ventilated by a continuous louvre) and the kitchen—a *jeu d'esprit* in the form of an imitation monastic kitchen (for example, that at Glastonbury) with a wooden roof finishing in a glazed lantern; sadly the lantern has now been dismantled but the room remains and is still the kitchen. The south wing, with the main entrance, belonged to the sisters and to 'penitents of a higher class of society'; the windows of the penitents' dormitory are plain, those of the sisters' foliated. The chapel (that is the early chapel, not to be confused with its magnificent successor) stands at the eastern end of this wing; formerly richly decorated, it is now bare and white-washed. The eastern side, closing the square, was simply a covered

Left, a close-up of the moulded brick frieze of the exterior—identical plaques arranged to make a lively floral pattern.

Right, a detail of the south side of the chapel, showing the wonderfully inventive use of brick-work. The mouldings of the parapet, windows, and buttresses have a crispness that would not be disdained by an architect of today. Even the drainpipes are fitted neatly into the design.

172

walk or cloister. Woodyer was particularly careful to ensure easy circulation under cover and his long corridors (usually gloomy affairs) are remarkably light and cheerful.

The material throughout is Woodyer's favourite red brick, meticulously used. The elevations are rich in surprising effects—in window arrangement, chimneys, projections and excrescences of every kind, reminiscent of Butterfield's sophistications at Rugby (for example, bay windows supported on flat buttresses). The later additions (of the '60s and '70s) include an extension of the western range to the south, an additional block between the west wing and the road, and more buildings to the north. At this end, separated from the convent by a garden, he had built in 1858 an orphanage for 25 children and 20 'industrial girls'. This, too, continued to grow, but the most interesting front is the first, with sharp narrow dormers, an equally spiky porch (now taken down) and an array of exotic chimneys swelling out from the first-floor walls and blossoming into long tapering shafts. Inside, Woodyer's most personal touches are his timber ceilings. That of the (early) chapel has an open ceiling on corbels with prettily turned beams; that of the orphanage chapel, which is otherwise plain enough, has a criss-cross arrangement of rafters, which reminds one, on a small scale, of E. B. Lamb, one of the wildest of Victorian 'rogue' architects.

The last crowning feature was the new chapel, built in 1881. Here Woodyer and Carter abandoned restraint and allowed themselves all the richness and colour that gratified their High Church instincts. It is not Woodyer's most extreme piece of originality (it has fewer eccentricities than, say, Christchurch, Reading), but it is a superb expression of Victorian confidence and must be one of the greatest feats of virtuoso brick-laying in England.

It consists of a short wide nave (rather like the ante-chapel of an Oxford college) and a narrower but equally high chancel. Both are on a grand scale, grander than strictly required by the numbers of the convent. The chancel was for the sisters, the nave for the other inmates. Nothing was spared to make an overwhelming impression; there are coloured marbles, polychrome masonry, terracotta panels, inlaid floor tiles, a profusion of carved woodwork and some extremely fine stained glass by Hardman (in the choir) and Clayton and Bell (in the nave).

The tall columns of the nave support a hammer-beam roof enriched by carving; aisles are as high as the nave and there is no clerestory. A carved oak rood screen and gallery separates nave from

A detail of the north wall of the chancel. The walls are of polychrome brick with terracotta plaques bearing the monogram of Christ. Corbels carved with naturalistic plants and animals support the vaulting shafts. The lower parts of the windows have been painted, the upper contain good stained glass by Hardman.

The interior of the nave, or antechapel, looking south. Woodyer excelled in grandiose timber roofs, and the brickwork is as interesting inside as out. Note the patterns made by the darker bands in the arches, the relation of header and stretcher alternating from triplet to triplet.

choir. Here the Butterfieldian polychromy is even more striking. The walls are decorated with diamond-shaped plaques bearing the monogram of Christ; the corbels of the 'vault' (which is in fact only a wooden imitation) each bear delightfully carved animals; while at the east end is a vast stone reredos full of tabernacle-work and figures by Nicholls, a popular church sculptor. Red brick is still the basic material, but for the doors and windows Woodyer used a dressing of red sandstone from Uttoxeter. Mullions are in moulded brick; tracery—a free version of Decorated—in stone.

The quality of the brickwork is best appreciated on the exterior. 'Wheeler Bros. of Reading have been the general contractors', states a contemporary account, 'and it would be difficult to find more excellent workmanship than they have produced.' The bricks are laid in English bond throughout, with the mortar on all vertical surfaces scraped out to leave the outlines sharp; on the sloping surfaces of the buttresses and the plinth at the base, however, the mortar is left flush with the bricks. On these sloping surfaces the bricks are laid at an angle, the layers dying into the horizontal courses further back—a device not peculiar to Woodyer but used by him to particularly good effect. Nook-shafts and mouldings of the windows are also in brick and there are delicately profiled brick eaves under the gutters. In the angles of the nave and choir on the south side is a bell turret, narrowing by stages as it ascends. To anyone climbing the spiral staircase inside for the first time, the effect of this narrowing is disconcerting. One suddenly reaches a point where the steps seem to rise vertically and the wall in front appears to arch over one's head.

Clewer became a centre for charitable work that spread far afield; there was even a mission to provide nurses for India. In the immediate vicinity, besides the orphanage, Woodyer built an extensive hospital or almshouse (complete with chapel and cloisters on the medieval model) and a villa for Carter, paid for by his admirers when he retired in 1880. Both these have been demolished within the last ten years. In 1926 the area west of the chapel was closed off into another quadrangle by two additional wings designed in an unobtrusive style by Cecil Hare. Otherwise Clewer is basically as Woodyer left it. He died in 1896, Carter in 1901.

The work of rescuing fallen women is no longer carried on there. The orphanage is a home for elderly ladies. The House of Mercy is now St John's Convent, where the sisters arrange retreats, make vestments and altar cloths and specialise in embroidery.

176

The rich, sombre colours of the chapel of the House of Mercy, Clewer, near Windsor, typify Victorian taste and Victorian piety; it typifies also Victorian philanthropy and Victorian imagination. For neo-Gothic, a style that suffers in our eyes from being so derivative, is handled by such architects as Henry Woodyer with a sincerity that makes it completely true to its own age. This view, from the west end, shows the nave with its timber roof, the choir screen and behind that the chancel.

CHAPTER 12

LA TOURETTE:
THE DOMINICANS IN THE MODERN WORLD

It was fitting that the Dominicans, probably the most progressive and modern-minded of all the orders, should have chosen Le Corbusier to build them a new convent. The actual decision was taken by the Dominican Chapter of Lyons but they were urged to do so by Father Couturier, a member of the order long concerned with the question of religious art, himself a painter, a friend of Matisse, Chagall and Braque, and one of Le Corbusier's warmest admirers, seeing him as 'one in whom the spontaneous sense of the sacred is most faithfully and strongly expressed'. He instructed him in the Dominican constitution; he fed him with suggestions and sketches; he made him visit the deserted Cistercian abbey of Le Thoronet to catch something of the atmosphere of devotion and permanence that was needed. He did all that a patron could do to help produce 'one of the purest and most significant architectural works of our time'.

Le Corbusier himself was deeply interested in the commission. A formative experience of his early years had been the Carthusian monastery of Ema, in Italy, which he had visited in 1911. It was here that he first conceived the idea of a *unité d'habitation* (which is certainly what a monastery is). He had been disappointed when, shortly after the Second World War, his scheme for a 20th-century hermitage, with an underground church, a hotel and hermits' cells on several storeys, had met with a discouraging response. But his highly individual pilgrimage church at Ronchamp had been universally acclaimed and, although an unbeliever and a man who in his past life had shown no conspicuous respect for any of the monastic virtues, he was discovering in himself (or others were discovering for him) an unsuspected vein of religious mysticism. When the project

178

for La Tourette was first suggested in 1953, he was 67 years old. His earlier 'Machine Age' style had given way to a more expressive and expressionist manner in which his favourite material, exposed concrete—*béton brut*—was moulded into shapes as evocative of the forms of nature as man. The proportions, window dispositions and so on, which often seemed entirely arbitrary, were in fact governed by a strict system, which he called the Modulor (short for *la module de la section d'or*), which is the Golden Section used in conjunction with the dimensions of the human body.

His clients, the Dominicans, friars of the Order of Preachers, live and work in the world, and monastic seclusion was not their prime requirement. They were founded at the same time as the Franciscans (St Dominic died in 1221), sharing with them the ideal of poverty and a sense of mission *in society*, and they have developed along roughly similar lines. Both shone in the schools and universities (the Dominicans produced St Thomas Aquinas) and both followed the explorers to every corner of the earth, spreading the faith and ministering to the newly converted. In the 16th and 17th centuries they were in charge of the Spanish Inquisition, developing later, with the Jesuits, into the Church's intellectuals *par excellence*. Today they retain both their single-mindedness and their high academic standards, keeping in the vanguard of scientific advance and rejecting nothing offered by modern techniques of communication.

Dominican churches were for long practically identical with those of the Franciscans. Most Italian cities have their San Francesco and San Domenico, big, barn-like structures, without aisles, usually roofed with timber, their plain walls covered in frescoes. The Dominican constitution contains no rules for building; it merely

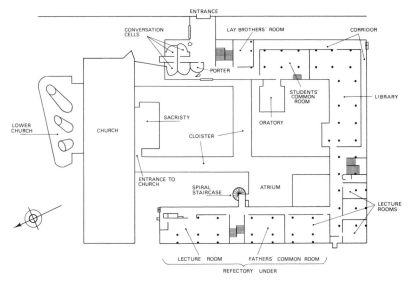

In the plan the following labels appear: ENTRANCE, CONVERSATION CELLS, LAY BROTHERS' ROOM, CORRIDOR, PORTER, STUDENTS' COMMON ROOM, LIBRARY, SACRISTY, ORATORY, LOWER CHURCH, CHURCH, CLOISTER, ENTRANCE TO CHURCH, SPIRAL STAIRCASE, ATRIUM, LECTURE ROOMS, LECTURE ROOM, FATHERS' COMMON ROOM, REFECTORY UNDER.

states that the order's needs are to be explained to a lay architect and the result left entirely to his discretion. This made the Dominicans probably the most amenable clients Le Corbusier ever had.

The community of Lyons already owned the plot of ground near Eveux-sur-l'Arbresle (north-west of Lyons) and an older convent, dating from the 19th century, stood near one side of it; they wanted new and enlarged accommodation, which was to include a residential theological college with a library and lecture rooms (this is the reason for its remote position in the country away from any large town). Le Corbusier chose a site some distance to the south of the older building with dense trees behind it to the east and a broad slope of open country to the west. Most Dominican convents had kept to the basic monastic pattern, with buildings grouped round three sides of a cloister, the fourth side being the church. Le Corbusier found no reason to vary this layout. He also preserved the feeling of an enclosed world, turned in upon itself. Like a Benedictine abbey or like a castle, La Tourette presents an impassive face to the outside.

La Tourette is basically a very simple building, though it is not easy to take in quickly because it is so tightly organised. It is planned in levels not in wings, and it will therefore be most convenient to describe it floor by floor rather than wing by wing; having done so we can more readily understand what happens in the central quadrangle, and finally look at the church, which stands on its own.

The entrance is on the east, a simple opening without gates or

With the Dominican convent of La Tourette, near Lyons, monastic architecture seems to have come a full circle. La Corbusier, of course, was anything but a simple architect, nor did he wish here to subdue his sophistication, but he created a building that had as direct an impact as Desiderius's Montecassino or St Bernard's Clairvaux. On the south side, shown opposite, the brothers' cells occupy the top storey, with the library and lecture rooms beneath them. 181

doors but with a free-standing 'arch' (two uprights and a lintel) to mark it symbolically. On the right are the porter's lodge and four conversation cells, the equivalent of the parlatorium. They are strange little rooms, with irregularly-spaced windows and curved walls somewhat reminiscent of Ronchamp, which stand isolated on a concrete platform, emphasizing their separateness from the convent proper. To the left of the entrance are a room for the lay brothers, a common room for novices and (turning the corner into the south wing) the library and reading room. All these rooms are lit by large windows arranged in a chequer-pattern looking on to the inner courtyard and are reached by a corridor running round the outer wall. Opening out from the novices' common room is a small oratory, an extraordinary conception, a stark concrete cube with a high pyramid roof jutting out into the courtyard area. There are no windows; the interior is lit by a shaft in the roof—a place of complete seclusion from the outside world.

At the end of the library (that is, in the middle of the south wing) the corridor switches from outer wall to inner wall and the remaining rooms to the south and west look out across the countryside. The movement is easily seen on the exterior, where the fenestration changes from the narrow strips needed to light the corridor to the tall vertical windows set at varying angles in close concrete mullions, which Le Corbusier called *pans de verre ondulatoires*. The rooms here are lecture and common rooms.

Underneath the west wing, where the drop in the ground allows the extra space, are the chapter room and refectory under which are

the kitchen and laundry, all lit in the same way. The refectory in particular is very light since it has windows on both sides. On the courtyard side of this wing is one of Le Corbusier's spiral staircases, climbing from kitchen to entrance-floor level.

The top two floors of all three wings are occupied by the cells, which provide accommodation for 100 friars. All the cells are the same. They are entered from a corridor on the courtyard side (again with the familiar slit windows); they have space for a bed, a table, and some book shelves and each leads, on the exterior, to a small balcony between windows.

The central courtyard is empty—Le Corbusier intended it to be part of the natural hillside landscape—but is crossed by covered and glazed passages on stilts, which are the 'cloister-walks' of La Tourette. Instead of following the sides of the square they cut across the middle in the form of a disjointed cross. The eastern arm leads in from the entrance; the northern leads to the church; the southern to the staircase of the library wing; and the western is opened out to form a spacious glazed area like a conservatory, called the 'atrium'. From here there is easy access to the other arms of the cloister and directly to the spiral staircase, the refectory and the chapter room. It is the informal meeting-place of the convent; the roof over it rises to a sharp angle, giving extra light.

The way the monastery is organised, once it is understood, is easily recognisable in the elevations. It is as functional, as economical and as neat as the aircraft and ocean liners that Le Corbusier so much admired. At the same time, his sense of volume, of light and

Above, the refectory, lit by long vertical windows on one side and chequer-board windows on the other. While the meal is in progress one of the brothers reads from some approved text.

Above left, a view inside the courtyard looking south-west: on the left the oratory, on the other two sides the south and west wings containing the main communal rooms. In the mid-foreground is the cross-shaped cloister, the high roof of the 'atrium' rising up where the four arms meet.

Opposite page, above, a view from the south-west. At the top are the friars' cells each with its balcony. Below them, on the south side (right), the corridor with its narrow horizontal windows gives way to the library, with generous vertical lights. On the west side two extra storeys are fitted in at the bottom—the refectory and kitchen. At the end is the west wall of the church.

Opposite page, below, the staircase tower attached to the west wing. It is a plain spiral staircase, its smooth curve contrasting with the rigid horizontals around it. The lower floor on the right is the refectory, the next, the fathers' common-room; the upper two are the corridors by which the cells are reached. 183

shade and of one space leading to another have never been more movingly displayed. One best qualified to have an opinion (that is, a Dominican, Father Illtud Evans) sees even more: 'It is the sense of common life, realised in peace and voluntary poverty, that dominates the priory . . . La Tourette must be judged one of the greatest sacred buildings of our time, and perhaps of any time.' He finds it particularly fitting for an order whose motto is the single word *Veritas*. Even so, on a more mundane level he concedes that the principle can be carried too far—the crudely exposed plumbing, for instance: 'the sound of many waters, so characteristic of most French buildings, is far from absent'.

The church is the most uncompromising and at the same time the most personal of all the parts of La Tourette. What the friars wanted was a building of some complexity: a large church for communal mass and choral services, a smaller church with several altars for individual masses, a sacramentary chapel (the Host is not kept permanently on the high altar of monastic churches), and a sacristy. As the main church Le Corbusier built a perfectly plain oblong box—184 in fact, not at all unlike the traditional Dominican church of the

Above, a view from the north-west. The rectangular box in the foreground is the church. Note the bell-turret, the lower church with its light-funnels, and the bulge to take the organ.

Right, an air-view from the south-west. Le Corbusier's whole design is conceived in terms of related geometrical shapes. Inside the main rectangle the pyramidal roof of the oratory stands out. Next to it is part of the cloister and towards the church, the sacristy with its seven 'light guns' aimed at the sun.

Above right, the interior of the church, with Mass in progress. The bare concrete of the walls is lined as if to give a hint of massive stone blocks.

Far right, the interior of the lower church. This contains all Le Corbusier's most expressive and dramatic features—coloured light from the circular shafts in the ceiling, curving walls, irregular levels and stark juxtaposition of concrete masses.

13th century. Externally the most striking features are the angular bell turret at the east end and a bulge at the west containing the organ. The roof is laid with turf to protect the concrete from sudden changes of temperature—an austere version, perhaps, of one of his famous roof gardens. Light enters the church from a variety of unexpected sources—from the sacristy and the chapel of the sacrament; from a square opening in the roof near the west end; from a narrow strip just under the eaves of the west end; from strips of window running along the north and south walls above the stalls to enable those taking part in the service to read; and from a vertical window running the whole height of the church in the south corner of the east wall. The interior is thus dimly but practically and imaginatively lit.

The smaller or lower church, reached by a passage going underneath the main one, bulges out from the north side in a strange bastion-like shape, lit from above by concrete funnels like the ventilators of a ship. (This has prompted some fanciful flights in the critics: 'the lower church of La Tourette is a submarine', says one, 'she has sunk out of the world, the light of which only reaches her from far away . . .') The funnels or 'light-guns' (*canons à lumière* as Le Corbusier calls them) are a particular and dramatic

feature of La Tourette. One of them is used to light the novices' oratory and seven more light the sacristy; but the three over the lower church take the idea furthest. Their inner surfaces are coloured white, red and black, so that the light changes in colour and intensity as the sun moves over them; the walls of the lower church are painted red and yellow, the ceiling blue. The floor, which is of large stones embedded in cement, follows the slope of the ground and the altars—concrete cubes and tables—are not in line but are staggered in an irregular rhythm. Over all the law of the Modulor reigns, producing a combination of excitement and repose exactly suited to the chapel.

La Tourette was begun in August 1956. The friars moved in on July 1, 1959. The church was consecrated on October 19, 1960. It has therefore been in existence for a very short time. Yet it is already a famous and much discussed building. In England reactions have varied from the 'high aesthetic line' to the down-to-earth professional. An example of the first may be taken from Colin Rowe in the *Architectural Review*: 'Since the coiled columnar vortex, implied by the space rising above the chapel, is a volume which, like all vortices, has the cyclonic power to suck less energetic material in towards its axis of excitement, so the three *canons à lumière* conspire with the elements guaranteeing hallucination to act as a kind of tether securing a tensile equilibrium.' And of the second from Alison Smithson: 'The building is like a stack of doughnuts . . . floors covered in bouncy green *Bulgomme Silence*. . . . The wash basins are so ghastly as to be almost refreshing . . . an absolute mine of cribs for the "proles".'

Le Corbusier has always been a mine of cribs. From La Tourette, the idea of a square turned in upon itself and showing a blank face to the outside world has been adapted to the alleged needs of a Cambridge hostel by Sir Leslie Martin; while in London, at Denys Lasdun's Royal College of Physicians, the submerged lecture theatre irresistibly recalls the lower church nestling against its high wall.

Le Corbusier's ideas will clearly be proliferated for years to come. What of the monastic ideal itself? No one can pretend that it plays more than a very marginal part in modern society. But it is not played out; it goes on adapting itself to an extent that few would once have foreseen. And it is, surely, significant that an architect of Le Corbusier's genius, a man moreover with such faith in the future, so deeply committed to revolutionising our houses, our cities and our lives, should have built La Tourette, and built it with such love and understanding. What next?

The bell-tower and cross over the east end of the church, a brilliantly lucid play of forms in Le Corbusier's mature style.

Further reading list

Aubert, Marcel, *L'architecture cistercienne en France*; Paris, 1947
Benedict, St, *The Rule of St Benedict* (several English translations)
Conant, Kenneth, *Carolingian and Romanesque Architecture;* Harmondsworth, 1959
Cranage, D. H. S., *The Home of the Monk*; London, 1926
Domenech y Montaner, Luis, *Historia y Arquitectura del Monasterio de Poblet*; Barcelona, 1928
Evans, Joan, *Monastic Life at Cluny*; London, 1931
Eydoux, H. P., *L'Architecture des eglises cisterciennes en Allemagne*; Paris, 1952
Gout, P., *Le Mont St Michel*; Paris, 1910
Henze, Anton, *La Tourette, The Le Corbusier Monastery*; London 1966
Sitwell, Sacheverell, *Monks, Nuns and Monasteries*; London, 1965

Glossary

apse: part of a building, usually the end of a chancel or chapel, that is semicircular in plan.

alternating supports: arcade in which the main piers alternate with less important subsidiary piers.

atrium: originally the courtyard of a Roman house. In Early Christian churches it is a rectangular arcaded courtyard in front of the main entrance.

barrel vault: continuous stone ceiling, either round or pointed in section.

capital: ornamental top of a column upon which the entablature rests.

clerestory: row of windows above the aisles, admitting light to the main body of a church.

cloister: an open space, normally rectangular, flanked on one side by the church and surrounded by covered walks, by which the principal parts of a monastery are reached.

Corinthian: the latest of the three classical Greek orders, distinguished by its capital formed of acanthus leaves.

crossing: the centre of a church where nave, chancel and transepts meet.

Decorated: a phase of English architecture, c. 1280–1340, characterised by complicated spatial effects, curvilinear tracery, ball-flower ornament and the ogee arch.

demi-column: a half-column embedded in a wall.

diaphragm arch: a masonry arch across a room or church that is otherwise roofed with timber.

groin vault: stone vault formed by the meeting of two barrel vaults at right angles, the edges not being strengthened with ribs.

infirmary: the hospital of a monastery, normally separate from the other buildings and with its own kitchen, chapel, etc.

intarsia: the art of making patterns or pictures by fitting together pieces of wood.

lancet: a tall narrow window without tracery, characteristic of early Gothic.

lantern: a covered and glazed opening in a roof to admit light.

lavatorium: place for washing, normally near the entrance to the refectory.

lintel: flat beam or slab resting on two uprights to form a door or window top.

loggia: an arcaded gallery open along one side.

lunette: the space between the lintel of an opening and the arch above it.

narthex: an enclosed porch in front of the main entrance to a church.

necessarium: latrine.

Perpendicular: phase of English architecture, c. 1340–1550, characterised by recti-linear tracery, blank panelling, four-centred arched and fan vaults.

pier: stone support of one side of an arch.

pulpitum: stone screen across the nave separating the monks' choir from the western part of a church.

putto (plural: **putti**): a cherubic naked boy.

reredorter: literally, 'behind the dormitory'. Monks' latrine.

retable: large painted or sculpted composition behind an altar.

rib vault: vault which is held together by an 'umbrella' of thin stone arches (ribs).

scriptorium: room in a monastery where manuscripts were copied and illuminated.

sexpartite vault: rib vault in which each bay is divided into six by two diagonal and one transverse arch; usually accompanied by alternating supports.

stucco: hard plaster, moulded into decorative or sculptural forms and whitewashed or painted.

trefoil: divided by cusps into three lobes.

undercroft: a basement room or rooms.

voussoirs: wedge-shaped stones forming an arch.

westwork: structure of several storeys, built at the west end of a church and usually opening on to the interior, mainly found in Carolingian and Romanesque Germany.

187

Index

Figures in italics refer to illustrations

Acknowledgements

The author and publishers wish to thank the Mother Superior and the Sisters of the Convent of St John the Baptist, Clewer, for their generous help and permission to reproduce drawings in their possession.

Key to picture positions: (*T*) top, (*B*) bottom, (*L*) left, (*R*) right. Numbers refer to the pages on which the pictures appear.

The pictures on pages 178, 179, 182, 184, 185, 186 photographed by Bernhard Moosbrugger, Zürich, taken with the permission of the original publishers from Henze/Moosbrugger *La Tourette The Le Corbusier Monastery;* copyright by Josef Keller Verlag, Starnberg/Germany, and Percy Lund, Humphries & Co. Ltd., London. The pictures on pages 141, 144(*R*), 145 taken from *Borromini, Architettura come linguaggio* by Paolo Portoghesi, published by Istituto Editoriale Electa, Milan, 1967. The pictures on pages 18, 31, are reproduced by permission of Professor Conant and the Mediaeval Academy of America. Other sources are as follows: Aerofilms 76(*L*); Archives Photographiques 73; Bavaria-Verlag 88(*BR*), 90, 91(*R*), 154, 156, 157(*R*), 161(*T*), 161(*R*); Bibliothèque Nationale 30; Bildarchiv Foto Marburg 14, 16(*R*), 19, 25, 33, 34, 79(*R*), 87, 88(*T*), 88(*BL*), 95, 142(*L*), 147, 150(*L*), 155, 157(*T*); Boudot-Lamotte 39, 44(*R*), 46(*L*), 46(*R*), 47, 78(*R*), 81, 82(*B*), 114(*TR*), 129(*TL*); British Museum endpapers, 4, 17, 140(*R*), 149, 150(*R*); British Travel Association 22(*L*); Camera Press 41; Connaissance des Arts 58, 59(*L*), 152; Courtauld Institute of Art 144(*L*); Deutsche Fotothek, Dresden 16(*L*), 26, 85, 92, 151; Kerry Dundas 77, 84; Fotocielo, Rome 140(*L*); French Government Tourist Office 63, 66; Giraudon 35, 51, 55(*L*), 56, 57; Lucien Hervé 62; Hirmer Fotoarchiv 153, 159, 160(*L*), 160(*R*); Michael Holford 166(*T*), 166(*B*), 167(*T*), 168, 169, 170, 171(*T*), 172, 175(*L*), 175(*R*), 177; Horst von Irmer 96; A. F. Kersting 21, 22(*R*), 24, 42(*L*), 43, 44(*L*), 45, 49, 80, 83, 158(*T*), 158(*B*), 163; Lossen Foto 8, 94; Mansell 129(*BL*); Mansell-Alinari 10, 113, 119(*R*), 125, 127, 130, 131, 146, 148; Mansell-Anderson 114(*TL*), 114(*B*), 115, 117(*L*); Mansell-Brogi 126, 129(*R*), 133(*R*); Ampliaciones y Reproducciones MAS 27, 99, 100, 101(*R*), 103(*L*), 103(*R*), 104(*T*), 104(*B*), 106, 107, 108; Leonard von Matt 112, 119(*L*), 120; Janine Niepce 65, 72(*L*), 72(*R*); Rapho 28, 60, 71(*T*), 101(*L*), 102, 180; Réalités 118; Jean Roubier 40, 42(*R*), 50, 54, 59(*R*), 61, 64, 67, 68, 69(*TR*), 69(*B*), 70, 71(*B*), 76(*R*), 78(*L*), 79(*L*), 82(*T*), 105, 117(*R*), 123(*L*), 123(*R*), 133(*L*); Scala 110, 135, 138; Helga Schmidt-Glassner 89, 91(*TL*), 91(*BL*), 93; Trinity College, Cambridge 20; Vatican Library 11.
189